DBT SKILLS WORKBOOK FOR TEENS

Unleash the Power of Dialectical Behavior Therapy to Regulate Emotions, Manage Anxiety, Improve Social Skills, and Practice Mindfulness

RESILIENT MINDS

TABLE OF CONTENTS

INTRODUCTION

"The path to healing begins with acceptance, not judgment."

- Marsha M. Linehan

Dialectical behavior therapy (DBT) is a therapeutic approach used to regulate emotions and help individuals navigate the complex challenges of their formative, growing years. Amid the increasing mental health crises among adolescents, DBT stands as a timely and crucial lifeline for teenagers dealing with mental health disorders. These disorders include anxiety, depression, low self-esteem, negative thinking, self-harming behaviors, and can even lead to suicidal thoughts. DBT offers a holistic approach to tackling these challenges, providing teens with essential tools and coping mechanisms to navigate their emotions and thoughts.

Adolescence is a stage characterized by rapid growth, complex transitions, and the development of personal identity. Teenagers emerge from a world of structured rules and guidance into one where they need to make their own decisions, establish their own values, and advocate for themselves. This transition is often accompanied by a heightened intensity of emotions, making this period one of the most emotionally challenging in a person's life. Truth be told, we have all been there ...

DBT for teenagers incorporates a unique dualistic approach—acceptance and change. While it might sound impossible and exhausting, it's not. The acceptance component encourages individuals to understand and acknowledge their experiences and emotions without judgment. This aids in developing self-compassion and reducing self-blame—a key element of healing and reviving change. The change aspect focuses on cultivating adaptive skills to manage their emotions, decrease negative thoughts, and improve relationships.

One of the fundamental principles of DBT is the belief that everyone is doing the best they can in their current circumstances. However, it also emphasizes the need for individuals to try harder and be more motivated to change. This paradoxical approach—promoting acceptance while encouraging change—reflects the dialectical philosophy inherent in DBT.

For adolescents like yourself, DBT is particularly beneficial because it provides concrete, actionable skills that will help you navigate the challenging emotional landscape. It not only gives you coping mechanisms but also empowers you to advocate for your own needs with your friends, parents, teachers, and everyone else in your life. This proactive approach boosts teenager's autonomy and self-confidence, fostering healthier relationships and more effective communication.

Through its dual approach of acceptance and change, DBT provides actionable tools to manage emotions, navigate relationships, and self-advocate. By involving families in the process, DBT creates a comprehensive treatment approach, establishing a nurturing environment for you to navigate your turbulent emotional landscape effectively, thereby fostering their overall mental well-being.

If you are reading this, I've got a feeling you might be going through a rough patch right now. It's okay; we all have those tough times. It's gut-wrenching how so many teens are struggling with their mental health. Trying to figure out and make your way through these teenage years can be really, really tough. It's like walking through an impossible maze of infuriating and overwhelming emotions.

Have you ever felt so frustrated and overwhelmed that you just wanted to scream, cry, or run away from everything? Yeah, we've all been there. School can be a real rollercoaster ride, with nothing going your way at times. Failing a test, getting teased for some random "uncool" t-shirt you wore, or having a falling out with friends can hit you hard. This is where DBT comes in—it's like a superhero for your emotional well-being. Remember that quote at the beginning of this introduction: "The path to healing begins with acceptance, not judgment?" This is the golden rule.

So, when life feels like it's pushing you to your limits, take a moment to pause and just breathe. Acknowledge and accept the emotions you're feeling. You do not need to judge yourself so harshly—just let those feelings be. Say to yourself, "I'm feeling anxious and depressed because of that test. I'm feeling uncomfortable and unhappy because of what they said about my shirt. I'm feeling really sad and lonely because of that fight with my friends." Don't let those feelings turn into a big mess of negativity. Just give them a name, accept them, and let go of any judgment. Trust me, it's a powerful way to start healing and finding your way through the tough stuff. You've got this! The whole concept of acceptance without judgment sits at the core of DBT.

During adolescence, you're likely to experience a whirlwind of emotions, intense relationships, and external pressures that can sometimes feel overwhelming. It's completely normal to struggle with feelings of confusion, frustration, anxiety, or even a sense of isolation during this phase of your life. In fact, it's important to know that you are not alone in this journey. It is equally important to know there are effective and easy-to-implement strategies available to help you build resilience, develop healthy coping mechanisms, and create a solid foundation for a fulfilling future.

Anxiety has so many faces that it's often hard to detect it. The most frequent face often appears as an intense sensation of fear that can disrupt your daily functioning, potentially causing difficulties in various aspects of life, including home, school, and relationships (Saripalli et al., 2021).

If you are anything like most of the teenagers in this world, then your answer is: "Yes, I have felt that way." Just look at the international superstar Selena Gomez herself. She experienced this all the time. It seemed like every time she turned around, there was drama. Either someone had said something untrue about her to the press, or someone else was critical of her, her weight, and her body, or someone else was picking on her for an outfit she had worn. Sound familiar? This is all the typical drama associated with being a teenager. Unfortunately for Selena, because she was so visible in the entertainment industry, it was magnified tenfold and widely reported. She knew she needed help, but she did not know what to do. Eventually, she tried DBT and has not looked back since. Selena credits it with saving her and helping her regain her mental health. It has been an absolute game-changer for her!

DBT also significantly helped another famous person that you are probably familiar with, Pete Davidson. Pete has openly talked in the press about how he turned to DBT out of desperation when he needed help trying to handle his discomfort and panic in social situations. He has spoken candidly about his challenges in trying to maintain relationships and comfortably participate in social situations. Pete was able to utilize the skills taught to him in DBT to feel better, control his emotions and impulses, and improve his relationships. I am telling you, DBT works!

So, what about you? What are you coping with? How are you feeling? Are you dealing with feeling overloaded? Do you feel overwhelmed with academic pressures and/or athletic performance expectations? Are your friends being difficult? Do you feel like an outsider? Are you having trouble controlling your anger? Do you feel anxious and depressed? Are you having trouble at home?

Are you ready to give DBT a try? Let's do it!

Throughout this book, you will be exposed to the DBT-LIFE method, which stands for:

DBT – Dialectical behavior therapy

L – Learn to be more aware of what's going on.

I – Increase control over your emotions.

F – Free yourself from being overwhelmed by stressful situations.

E – Establish positive relationships using improved communication skills.

Dialectical Behavior Therapy (DBT) Skills Workbook for Teens is an essential resource designed to give teenagers like you the tools and strategies needed to navigate the often tumultuous journey of adolescence. This book is a comprehensive and practical guide that will introduce you to the transformative power of dialectical behavior therapy—a proven therapeutic approach tailored specifically to address the unique challenges faced by teenagers in today's fast-paced and complex world.

I want you to understand, as you read this, that every word you read and every page you turn in this book brings you a step closer to finding true peace with yourself, your thoughts, and your surroundings. This really could be the answer you've been searching for—yes, it really could. DBT is a powerful therapy designed for teenagers, just like you, who are facing mental health challenges. With its unique combination of acceptance and change, DBT provides you with practical tools to handle emotions, navigate relationships, and stand up for what you need. And the best part? It's not a solo journey; DBT brings your friends, family, and anyone you choose to include in your life together to create a supportive and nurturing environment. It's like a complete package for your emotional well-being, paving the way for a happier and healthier you.

DBT can be intricate and multifaceted; this book presents the information to you in a straightforward and approachable manner, enabling you to comprehend and implement DBT skills and concepts effectively.

But why should you pick this book? Because it consists of firsthand experiences and accounts of teens who use it in their lives and how it changed their lives for the better. By the time you're done with this book, you will be able to live a fulfilling life unhindered by stress, negativity, and other issues.

Remember, this journey is not about perfection but rather about progress. Each step you take toward implementing DBT principles and practicing the skills provided in this book brings you closer to a healthier, happier, and more authentic version of yourself. Embrace this opportunity to discover your inner strength, cultivate meaningful relationships, and lay the foundation for a future filled with resilience and self-empowerment.

So, let's embark on this transformative journey together!

CHAPTER 1:

DIALECTICAL BEHAVIOR THERAPY

"Emotions are not good, bad, right, or wrong. The first step to changing our relationship to feelings is to be curious about them and the messages they send to us."

- Lane Pederson

This is an incredible quote, and I want you to focus on it because of its importance and relevance. Lane quotes that "emotions are not good, bad, right, or wrong." Before we explore the actual meaning of it, read it twice and let that sink in.

What does that mean? In the realm of healing and personal growth, Lane Pederson's wisdom mirrors the profound words of Marsha Linehan on acceptance. Remember Linehan's quote? "The path to healing begins with acceptance, not judgment." In essence, Lane Pederson is saying to accept your emotions for whatever they are. They are not good, bad, right, or wrong; they simply are. Accept them.

What we feel should never be a subject of morality; otherwise, it takes away from it. Our emotions are neurological messengers from our minds that shouldn't be ignored.

In this chapter, we will explore four fundamental elements that form the backbone of DBT. These key components will help you grasp the unique philosophy and approach that DBT brings to the table. By delving into these four crucial parts, you will gain a deeper appreciation for the power of DBT as a therapeutic tool for personal growth, emotional well-being, and navigating life's challenges.

So, before we embark on this transformative journey, let's take a moment to explore the basics of DBT, which will serve as guideposts, illuminating the path ahead and giving you a glimpse into the profound impact that DBT can have on your life.

Here is a little background on the origin of DBT.

Marsha Linehan, the brilliant mind behind dialectical behavior therapy (DBT), crafted this therapeutic approach on a powerful belief: that both acceptance and change can peacefully coexist to bring about a positive state of mind. Linehan's research led her to a profound realization encompassing two seemingly contradictory yet equally essential concepts in the realm of mental health:

Firstly, to lead fulfilling and contented lives, individuals must learn to accept things as they are—embracing the present moment without judgment. Secondly, change is vital for personal growth and happiness, driving us forward toward a better future (Linehan, 2016).

Many individuals grappling with mental health issues perceive life in black-and-white terms or adhere to an "either-or" mentality (Onque, 2023). DBT aims to find balance and the middle ground, embracing the idea of "both-and" for a more comprehensive perspective. For example, Jack has been struggling with extreme emotions, negative thinking, and depression since childhood, so he often experiences intense emotions and tends to view situations as extremes (e.g., all good or all bad; right or wrong). Through DBT, he learned to embrace dialectics and find a middle ground.

For instance, he may recognize that a person can have both positive and negative qualities or that a situation can have both challenges and opportunities. Let me give you a relatable experience on this. You want to excel academically and get good grades, but you also crave social interactions and fun experiences, so you are struggling to maintain a balance, right?

Dialectics encourages you to find a middle ground between these two aspects of your life. You can acknowledge the importance of studying and putting effort into your education while also making time for socializing and enjoying the company of your friends.

Rather than feeling torn between academic success and social life, you can learn to strike a balance that allows you to both excel in your studies and build meaningful relationships. Dialectics in this context helps teens accept that both aspects are valuable and necessary for their overall well-being, enabling them to create a fulfilling and balanced teenage experience.

This shift in perspective helped Jack find balance and make more nuanced judgments.

Depression and anxiety in teens remain the most underdiagnosed and mishandled mental health conditions. DBT stands out as an effective way to help teens accept themselves and heal their wounds.

DBT's essence lies in teaching and providing individuals with four fundamental skills that are essential for personal growth and well-being, specifically. These four skills make up the foundation of DBT, which are mindfulness, distress tolerance, interpersonal communication, and emotional regulation (Schimelpfening, 2023).

DBT's Specialty, Dialectics

The term "dialectical" in therapy stems from the belief that combining two opposing elements, *acceptance and change,* leads to more favorable outcomes compared to either one in isolation. Teenagers like yourself absolutely thrive in this environment, so let's create an atmosphere of acceptance and encourage change in it.

DBT places great importance on accepting an individual's experiences without any judgment to provide reassurance while also addressing the necessary work to modify negative behaviors. For example, if a teen is struggling with low self-esteem and turning to self-harming behaviors as a way to cope with their emotions. They feel overwhelmed by negative thoughts about themselves and are experiencing intense emotional pain.

In DBT, a compassionate and non-critical environment would be created for them to express their feelings and experiences surrounding their self-esteem struggles and self-harm. They will be listened to actively and provided with reassurance that the teen's feelings are valid and understood.

They will also receive recognition that their self-harming behaviors are a response to emotional pain and a coping mechanism they have adopted. Further, they would encourage change and help the teen to conquer their self-harming behavior, and instead, substitute a better, healthier option. The focus would be on acknowledging and accepting these experiences without judgment, emphasizing that it is okay to feel the way they do.

At the same time, the DBT team/therapist, friends, family, and school members would work with the teen to explore healthier ways to cope with their emotions and build self-esteem. They might teach the teen mindfulness techniques to manage upsetting emotions, encourage self-compassion exercises, and offer alternative coping strategies like journaling or seeking support from trusted friends or family members.

By combining acceptance and validation of the teen's experiences with guidance on more positive coping strategies, DBT empowers the teen to work toward healing and self-improvement. The teen feels understood and supported while also gaining tools to overcome their struggles and develop a more positive and resilient outlook. This approach fosters a sense of hope and a path toward positive change and emotional well-being.

As you progress through this book and learn the skills associated with each of the four main tenets of DBT: Mindfulness and meditation, Distress tolerance, Emotion regulation, and Interpersonal effectiveness, you will be asked to complete activities or homework assignments aimed at practicing new skills.

Homework Assignments? I know; I know it sounds like school, but trust me, it's not. These assignments are nothing like your daily homework, which is crammed with math problems and equations. DBT exercises and assignments are much more practical and easily applicable to your daily life. A very common assignment may involve completing daily "diary cards" to help you identify, label, and monitor over 40 emotions, urges, behaviors, and skills, such as dishonesty, self-harm, or self-esteem (Taylor, 2022). These assignments are relatively straightforward and very manageable. And remember, they are designed to help you understand your emotions and how you can interpret each one of them effectively to improve your life and mental state.

The Hype of DBT

There has been a lot of buzz around DBT in the past few years. As our society becomes increasingly aware of mental health and its importance, people every day scout for ways they can either improve it or heal from any traumatic incidents. Naturally, DBT receives a lot of hype, and for all the right reasons. Obviously, since it's been trending on TikTok, there is a lot of dancing involved, but in reality, DBT has nothing to do with that; instead, it has changed the course for many teens and individuals around the world, all by simple, uncomplicated steps.

It's remarkable, actually, how instantaneously DBT has become a sensation. In the relatively short period it has been around, DBT has shown its effectiveness in treating and managing various mental health conditions that were previously considered difficult to treat. It's like a game-changer, offering hope and progress for conditions that had limited options before, such as anxiety, PTSD, and eating disorders. While there are several benefits of DBT, I wanted to highlight a few prominent ones to give you an idea of what it can do for you. The major advantages include:

Acceptance and Change

In DBT, you'll learn strategies for embracing and enduring your situations in life, your emotions, and yourself. You will also be able to highlight skills that will enable you to influence positive changes in your actions and interactions with others (Schimelpfening, 2023).

Behavioral

You'll gain the ability to assess problems or harmful behavior patterns and replace them with healthier and more effective alternatives. You'll develop the skills to analyze and address these issues in a way that promotes positive change and fosters personal growth (Eddins, 2017).

Cognitive

A key focus is on modifying thoughts and beliefs that are ineffective or negative. You'll learn strategies to identify and challenge negative or distorted thinking patterns and work toward adopting more constructive and beneficial thoughts and beliefs (Schimelpfening, 2023). This process of cognitive change can have a significant impact on your overall well-being and ability to navigate life's challenges more effectively.

Collaboration

Most importantly, you'll develop the skills to communicate effectively and collaborate as a team with your therapist, group therapist, or anyone else you want to include. You'll learn techniques for expressing yourself clearly, actively listening to others, and fostering a cooperative and supportive environment (Eddins, 2017). By working together as a cohesive unit, you can enhance the effectiveness of your treatment and create a strong foundation for personal growth and progress.

Skill Sets

Skills enable us humans to survive and thrive in this world. Throughout your experience, you will be introduced to a range of new skills that aim to enhance your capabilities. These skills will encompass various areas, such as emotion regulation, distress tolerance, interpersonal effectiveness, and mindfulness (Eddins, 2017).

Support

Support is a huge factor in the whole DBT approach. Throughout your journey, you will receive encouragement to acknowledge and embrace your positive strengths and attributes. The therapy will focus on helping you identify these qualities within yourself and further develop and utilize them in your life. By recognizing and leveraging your positive strengths, you can enhance your self-esteem, build resilience, and maximize your potential for personal success and fulfillment (Schimelpfening, 2023).

When you start your journey toward healing and reconciling with yourself, DBT will not only aid you in the whole process but will act as your safety net.

What Is DBT Used For?

One of the best things about DBT is that it is so applicable to the many issues and stressors associated with being a teenager. Learning and implementing DBT skills and strategies has been proven to help with:

- Attention-deficit/hyperactivity disorder (ADHD)
- Bipolar disorder
- Borderline personality disorder (BPD)
- Eating disorders (such as anorexia nervosa, binge eating disorder, and bulimia nervosa)
- Generalized anxiety disorder (GAD) (Schimelpfening, 2023)
- Major depressive disorder (including treatment-resistant major depression and chronic depression)
- Non-suicidal self-injury (Self-harm)
- Obsessive-compulsive disorder (OCD)
- Post-traumatic stress disorder (PTSD) (Cleveland Clinic, 2022)
- Substance use and abuse
- Negative thinking
- Low self-esteem

- Social anxiety
- Suicidal behavior (Schimelpfening, 2023)

Hannah's Story

It started off as anxiety, which amplified, and it turned into depression without her realizing what was happening to her. It affected her schoolwork, relationships, and sleeping patterns. She felt inadequate among her friends, frustrated by them, and paranoid that they were upset with her. Her relationship with her family also deteriorated immensely, as she would lash out at her siblings and parents. She had the urge to scream at people and often gave into it. For instance, this one time, she was studying in a classroom with her friends, and they were being really loud. So she started screaming at them to the point that they were taken aback. Hannah's mom was an active supporter of therapy, which is why she agreed to try DBT.

Instead of teaching her how to live a perfect life, DBT therapy taught her how to cope with everyday problems in life. To accept who you are as a person. Not to try changing who you are. It also helped her learn ways to deal with the problems in her life, which made it easier for her to navigate. Eventually, little by little, Hannah started recovering and doing better for herself. That is DBT for you—not a quick fix but rather a slow process toward active healing.

Final Words...

Now you know that you are not alone in your feelings, not by a long shot. Very few people, if any, make it through their teenage years without struggling to a degree with mental health issues. Celebrities like Selena and Pete and regular teenagers like Jack and Hannah have all struggled the same way you are. And now you know real help is available to you and that it works!

DBT has some promising results. It is relatively easy to learn and directly applicable to your life. It can enable you to regain control of your life through acceptance and collaboration. While it was originally developed to treat BPD, it has now become a staple in the treatment of numerous other mental health conditions, such as depression and anxiety. We are going to delve into all the details of DBT and how to practice it in this book; we will walk you through it. But first, we need to look at stress. So, why are teens so stressed out? Keep reading to find out!

CHAPTER 2:

IT'S A HARD-KNOCK LIFE: HERE'S WHY YOU FEEL STRESSED ALL THE TIME

"And still, I rise."

- Maya Angelou

Have you ever felt like you don't know why you feel angry? Or that you lost your temper without any definitive trigger? Have you ever found yourself losing your temper with someone, even when the situation didn't really call for it? Or do you sometimes struggle to respond proportionally to a situation and end up having a full-blown meltdown? Hey, you're not alone—these things happen a lot, especially during the teenage years. Even celebrities go through these challenges, too. It's all part of being human, and it's totally okay!

Remember Selena Gomez?

In 2022, she revealed that she was diagnosed with bipolar disorder, depression, and anxiety. It makes you wonder: how can someone like Selena have such an amazing career and life and yet still suffer and struggle? How can it be possible that one of the most popular, beautiful, and talented people on the planet feels so overwhelmed and anxious? Well, Selena's battle with stress and anxiety started when she was a teenager … No one escapes the tumultuous ups and downs of adolescence and stress. Selena kept her mental health conditions to herself until she found DBT and received great comfort and relief by practicing the same skill you will learn in this book. Yes, it's true; Selena Gomez credits DBT with significantly improving and helping her mental health. In an interview with Vogue Australia, she said, "I've studied DBT, which is dialectical behavior therapy, and I feel like I practice [DBT] every day."

She later went on to include that it had changed her life (Jacoby, 2021). And all for the right reasons. Don't you think Selena looks happier in her TikTok and music videos?

Much like Selena, many teenagers around the world, maybe even yourself, struggle with mental health issues that, if left untreated, can become a barrier preventing you from reaching your true potential. This chapter explores the reasons why you feel so overwhelmed and stressed out and why DBT is a very effective and applicable modality for people your age. At the end of this chapter, you will come to appreciate DBT and relate to it a little more.

The Root of Stress

You are already aware of the growing numbers of depressed and anxious teens. It is truly heartbreaking how our new generation is pushed into self-destructive patterns and mental health conditions. Often, teens feel like a misfit, alienated from the crowd and their peers. According to the 2017 Children Mental Health Report, anxiety disorders are the most common mental health condition to affect teenagers (Steinberg, 2021). For example, at the age of only 13, 8% of US teens have a diagnosable anxiety disorder. Similarly, by the age of 18, up to 15% of all teens experience symptoms of a clinical anxiety disorder (ADAA, 2009). In fact, in research done by Pew, 7 out of 10 teenagers claim that anxiety and depression are a common denominator of stress amongst their peers (ADAA, 2009). Aside from all the depressive episodes and panic attacks, as you grow older, you realize that whatever you felt in your teens had long-lasting effects. This begs an important question—why do these conditions exist or occur in teens?

It all goes back to acceptance and judgment. Teens are excessively critical of their appearances and their stances in society; hence, they struggle with accepting themselves, their flaws, and their mistakes. But why do they get depressed and anxious? If you want to consider a short answer—life is hard. But, if you want an elaborate answer, most of this depression stems from traumatic childhood experiences, toxic environments, and unwanted pressure, whether it is related to academics or peer pressure. So, stress is caused by many underlying factors that not only contribute to its existence but also add to depression and anxiety within a teen's life.

Causes of Stress

Stress is a common factor when it comes to teens and their mental health issues. While many of them are depressed and anxious, they are equally stressed out. Before you dive into how DBT can effectively curb any such issues, it's important to understand the underlying causes of such issues so that you can weed out every bit of it on your journey toward recovery. Here are 9 main causes of stress in a teen's life:

1. Academic Pressure

Teens often experience stress due to the demands of their academic responsibilities. For example, they may feel anxious about upcoming exams, deadlines for assignments, or the need to maintain high grades to meet parental or societal expectations.

2. Peer Pressure

Social pressures from peers can be a significant source of stress for teenagers. For instance, they may feel pressured to engage in risky behaviors such as smoking a cigarette or drinking alcohol.

3. Family Expectations

Expectations from parents and family members can create stress for teenagers. For example, the pressure to excel in specific subjects, pursue certain career paths, or uphold family traditions can be overwhelming.

4. Hormonal Changes

During adolescence, hormonal fluctuations can impact teens' emotions and mood, leading to stress. For instance, sudden mood swings or heightened sensitivity to stressors may be related to hormonal changes.

5. Body Image Concerns

Teenagers may experience stress and anxiety related to body image issues. For example, comparing themselves to unrealistic beauty standards portrayed in the media can cause stress about their appearance.

6. Transition and Changes

Significant life transitions, such as moving to a new school or dealing with parental divorce, can be stressful for teens. Adjusting to a new environment or coping with changes in your family dynamics can contribute to stress.

7. Peer Relationships

Friendship dynamics and conflicts with peers can cause stress for teenagers. For instance, experiencing social exclusion or dealing with rumors and gossip can lead to emotional stress. Most importantly, teens during this time might deal with bullying. This is the main cause of a lot of stress and low self-esteem.

8. Time Management

Juggling academic responsibilities, extracurricular activities, and social commitments can be challenging for teens and may result in stress. For example, feeling overwhelmed by a busy schedule and struggling to find time for extracurriculars can cause stress.

9. Future Uncertainties

As teenagers plan for their future, they may feel stressed about making important decisions. For instance, choosing the right college or career path can create anxiety about the unknown. While these are some of the factors that aid stress in a teen's life, there is a specific contributor that has become increasingly popular recently. Can you guess it? Yes, social media!

Social Media & Stress

It goes without saying that social media has become a huge part of everyone's lives, including teenagers. So, here's the big question: Are teens and social media a good mix, or does social media use actually lower teen well-being? It's a hot topic these days, and there are studies with mixed results that add to the debate.

According to a recent report by Common Sense Media on the effects of social media on teens, about half of the 1,500 young people surveyed find social media very important. They use it to get support and advice and to feel less alone. It's a creative outlet for them, and it helps them stay connected with friends and family. In fact, 43 percent said that using social media makes them feel better when they're feeling down, stressed, or anxious. For LGBTQ youth, that number goes up to 52 percent, showing that social media can be a source of comfort during tough times.

But, of course, there's another side to the story. The report also revealed a strong link between social media and teens feeling depressed. Teens with moderate to severe depressive symptoms were almost twice as likely to be constant social media users. One-third of depressed teens reported using social media almost constantly, compared to only 18 percent of those without depressive symptoms. And here's the kicker: the more severe their symptoms, the more anxious, lonely, and depressed they felt after using social media. It's clear that for teens who are already feeling down, social media isn't helping and may even contribute to their negative feelings.

How does social media adversely impact teens?

Social media is not all bad, but it is widely fake. Now, that seems like a big claim, but it is not completely wrong. Throughout these platforms, posts present carefully curated and idealized versions of people's lives. Teens may compare themselves to others and feel inadequate when they perceive that others have more exciting lives, better looks, or greater achievements. This constant social comparison can lead to feelings of insecurity and stress. For example, young teenage girls might stumble onto a post by Instagram influencers who have edited and drastically changed their bodies. This not only sets unrealistic beauty standards but also thrusts young girls into the trap of insecurities and low self-esteem. Aside from the constant comparison, teens might become victims of negative comments, body shaming, and cyberbullying on social media, especially related to body size, shape, or appearance. Such hurtful remarks can deeply affect a teen's self-image and self-worth. However, not all is lost—social media has its perks as well. For example, it can also be a platform for body positivity and self-acceptance. Influencers such as Lizzo, Billie Eilish, etc., and organizations promoting body diversity and acceptance have provided and continue to provide teens with a more inclusive and empowering perspective on body image.

So, while social media can be a helpful tool for many teens, it's essential to keep an eye on how it impacts your well-being. If you find yourself constantly comparing your life and body to those on the internet, log off, delete your account, or take a break. As with everything, finding a healthy balance is key when it comes to social media.

With that being said, stress is a part of life; therefore, if you are able to identify the main causes and triggers, you will also be able to diffuse them.

Have you ever felt so overwhelmed that you would cry the minute something went sideways? That's exactly how Emily felt. With complex and advanced courses, extracurricular activities, and high expectations from her parents, Emily often found herself struggling to keep up.

One particularly stressful week, Emily had three major exams, a debate competition, and a piano recital, all scheduled back-to-back. She felt the weight of the world on her shoulders as she tried to balance her academic responsibilities with her extracurricular passions (My Health Alberta, 2019).

As the pressure mounted, Emily's stress began to take a toll on her well-being. She experienced difficulty sleeping, a lack of appetite, and a constant feeling of restlessness. She could feel her health and happiness slipping away, but she didn't know how to break free from the cycle of stress.

Recognizing the severity of her situation, Emily finally reached out for support. She confided in her close friends, who provided a listening ear and offered advice on managing stress. Emily also sought guidance from her school counselor, who helped her develop healthy coping mechanisms such as time management strategies, relaxation techniques, and seeking support from teachers. This allowed her to manage her stress effectively. This is a prime example of a teen experiencing stress while in school.

Now, in the case of Emily, she was stressed because of the academic pressure, as she was unable to juggle everything that was on her plate. So, stress arises when one faces demands beyond one's accustomed capacity. It is a common experience for most teenagers, impacting individuals in varied ways. What induces stress in you may not evoke the same response in someone else. But, there are some common triggers that can all elicit stress, such as taking a test, delivering a class presentation, or preparing for a sports competition.

Long-Term & Short-Term Stressors

Have you ever felt butterflies in your stomach before taking a test or going on stage to give a performance? Or has your heartbeat accelerated when your teacher asked you a question? These are classic indicators of stress. Naturally, when you are caught off guard by a teacher's question or nervous about a performance during your talent show, your body deals with a process called "short-term" stress.

Short-term stress is normal in many cases and can even be beneficial. It can motivate you to work hard or respond swiftly. For instance, stress can be advantageous in completing important tasks within deadlines. However, when it becomes persistent, it begins to create problems in your life. The "fight or flight" response triggered by short-term stressors helps the body prepare for physical threats. It increases alertness, focus, and physical readiness to deal with potential danger. Similarly, it can promote adaptation and learning. Whenever you face and overcome challenges, you develop resilience and coping skills that can benefit you in future situations. For example, managing to prepare for a tricky exam enables you to absorb knowledge and stabilize your focus on what is important. These are skills that help you in your professional career when you have to meet deadlines on short notice.

Long-term stress emerges from enduring stressful circumstances or events. What are these triggers? Overachieving attitude. Now, don't get me wrong, sometimes it's an active motivator, but usually, when you exert pressure on yourself to excel academically, stress becomes an active participant in your life. Moreover, experiencing negative body image or self-esteem or encountering difficulties within the family or with parents are situations that create a toxic environment, which in turn results in stress and anxiety. Extended periods of stress can have detrimental effects on your health, especially your mind (My Health Alberta, 2019). Here are 7 main long-term stress triggers that you need to look out for:

1. Chronic Health Conditions

Dealing with a chronic health condition, such as diabetes, asthma, or allergies, can be a long-term stressor. Managing the condition, coping with symptoms, and adjusting to lifestyle changes can create ongoing stress.

2. Personal Trauma

Experiencing trauma, such as physical or emotional abuse, can lead to prolonged stress and post-traumatic stress disorder (PTSD). For example, a teen might experience long-term stress due to the car accident that they witnessed or were a part of; this leads them to have severe anxiety and stress.

3. Relationship Issues

Troubled or dysfunctional relationships, such as demanding parents or strained friendships, can be ongoing stressors. For instance, a teen who comes from a household prone to domestic abuse or emotional abuse might suffer from chronic stress. Ongoing family conflicts, such as parental divorce, domestic disagreements, or strained relationships with family members, can create long-term stress for teens.

4. Living in Challenging Environments

Living in unsafe neighborhoods, areas affected by natural disasters, living with financial uncertainty, or experiencing homelessness can lead to chronic stress and uncertainty.

5. Body Image and Appearance Pressures

Constant comparison with societal beauty standards and the desire to fit in with perceived body ideals can cause ongoing stress. For example, a teen might be struggling with body dissatisfaction due to expectations of a particular body shape or size among their peers and/or society. Social media has a huge role to play in this. As discussed earlier, social media aids, if not creates. the whole misconception of "ideal body types." Our bodies come in different shapes and sizes, so it's important to remember that everyone is beautiful just the way they are.

6. Cultural and Identity Stress

Teens from diverse backgrounds may experience long-term stress due to cultural conflicts, identity struggles, or discrimination. Teens who are multiracial or come from different ethnicities might feel torn between adhering to traditional cultural values and fitting into the broader societal norms. As a result, they feel like an imposter amongst their peers, alienated and alone.

7. Feeling Less Than

Teenagers often find themselves caught up in the habit of comparing their lives to those of others—whether it's their friends, classmates, celebrities, or influencers. This can sometimes leave them feeling like they're not quite measuring up. You know how it goes, right? They see Johnnie cruising into school in a shiny new car, and suddenly, their own mode of transportation feels a bit less exciting. Or maybe they spot Jasmine rocking the latest designer outfits, and it's hard not to wish for a wardrobe makeover.

But hey, here's the thing: we've all been there. It's easy to forget that what we see on the surface doesn't always reflect the whole story. So, if you ever catch yourself playing the comparison game, just remember that your journey is unique, and the best way to measure your worth is by the experiences you collect and the person you're becoming.

Now, this might make you wonder how stress impacts your brain.

Our mind is the hub of the whole nervous system that runs throughout our body, and stress is a response in the face of perceived danger or fear; hence, the butterflies in your stomach during a test. So, how does it work? Well, when you are in danger or under threat, your body and brain trigger a surge of stress hormones, including adrenaline and cortisol. These hormones activate the part of the nervous system known as the sympathetic nervous system, also called the stress response or "fight-or-flight" reaction. During a dangerous situation, have you ever felt like you were invincible? That is famously termed an "adrenaline rush."

Signs of Stress

Now, you already know that stress works differently in adults compared to teens. Since stress can mimic normal teenage hormonal changes in teens, it's harder to pinpoint.

However, there are certain prominent signs that you can keep in mind, which include:

Headaches and Stomachaches

Physical health issues are frequently brought on by stress. Persistent headaches, stomachaches, and other physical complaints can be indicators of stress (Morin, 2020).

Sleep Issues

Difficulty in falling asleep or maintaining a sleep schedule can indicate the presence of stress. Moreover, this can contribute to a detrimental mental health cycle. When a teenager is excessively fatigued, they become less resilient to stress, so a little bit more of an academic load, and they experience breakdowns.

Certain stressed teens may exhibit excessive sleep patterns. For instance, a teenager who constantly desires to return to bed after school or attempts to sleep excessively during weekends might be utilizing sleep as a means to evade their stress.

Educational Problems

Oftentimes, school-related problems such as academic pressure and extracurriculars can be a root cause of stress-related disorders. For example, a change in a teen's attendance or declining grades is an active indicator of stress.

Increased Irritability

Teens are moody by nature, but if one of them is having sudden outbursts in the middle of a lecture, then something is definitely wrong. A stressed-out teen is likely to be more irritable than usual. A teen who becomes irritable over small inconveniences frequently may be feeling overwhelmed by life's challenges.

Changes in Socialization

Naturally, teens are eager to socialize and make friends. They are on the verge of affirming their personalities. Whether extroverted or introverted, they are finding their place, but if stress has different plans for them, that can become a long-term problem. Stress has the potential to alter the social behavior of teenagers. One possible indication that a teen is grappling with stress is their inclination toward social isolation. This can manifest as spending increased amounts of time in their room or displaying a lack of enthusiasm for engaging with friends, suggesting that the teenager is encountering difficulties.

Frequent Illness

Stress can make you get sick repeatedly. Teens who are stressed out are often sick with colds, flu, and other minor illnesses. They miss school or social events, and their grades suffer.

Negative Changes in Behavior

When a teenager experiences stress, it frequently leads to behavioral issues. These problems can encompass a wide range, including school truancy and disrespectful behavior. However, it is important not to justify negative behavior solely on the grounds that it is stress-related. While stress can contribute to these behaviors, it is crucial to address them appropriately rather than dismissing them outright (Morin, 2020).

Difficulty Concentrating

When teens have a lot on their minds, it's hard for them to concentrate on their work. They may become easily distracted in class and have increased difficulty staying on task while completing their homework.

Negative Talk

Stressed teenagers frequently employ negative language as a way of expressing their emotions. For instance, they might make statements like "Nobody likes me" or "Everything always goes wrong." While occasional use of such comments is considered normal for teens, if you notice an excessive repetition of these negative expressions, it is likely an indication of heightened stress levels (Morin, 2020).

General Sense of Worry

Teens experiencing stress often find themselves consumed by worries that extend to various aspects of their lives. They may become preoccupied with potential negative outcomes or fixate on how they are being perceived by others (Morin, 2020). If a teen has been exhibiting an increased level of worry beyond their usual patterns, it is likely a result of heightened stress.

Here are some tips to be on the lookout for that might indicate you are experiencing a heightened level of stress:

- Fatigue
- Being disengaged
- Being anxious or panicky
- Being depressed
- Headaches or stomach aches
- Irritability
- Difficulties with concentration and focus
- Changes in appetite
- Increased use of alcohol or drugs
- Withdrawal from family or friends
- Loss of interest in hobbies (ReachOut Parents, 2020)

While these signs can be confusing, it's always important to be mindful of what people around you are going through.

The Truth ...

Did you know that 7 out of 10 people struggle with their mental health? In a recent survey commissioned by the National 4-H Council, it was discovered that during the wake of the pandemic, 60–70% of teens around the world were struggling with their mental health (PR Newswire, 2020).

In fact, more than half of the surveyed teens shared that they feel pressure to hide their feelings, and they want that to change. So, it's safe to say that you are not alone. Jennifer Sirangelo, the president and CEO of the National 4-H Council, emphasized the responsibility of acknowledging and addressing the unique world and challenges faced by young people today (PR Newswire, 2020). She described a survey as a crucial window into the uncertainties that many teenagers experience on a daily basis. Teens worldwide experience stress and anxiety because of the growing pressure and expectations. If you feel like the stress is out of hand—consider seeking help from professionals.

Plus, the truth is that we are all dealing with something in our lives. I'll give you some important advice that I have learned and something you'll see plastered over Facebook (not Instagram; this isn't a motivational video): find yourself a friend who you can rely on and stick with them. When things get tough, lean on them a little bit. It's natural for human beings to try and find comfort during hard times; do not deny yourself the warmth of companionship.

Triggers of Stress

So, let's understand why you become stressed.

There are several triggers, but I want to discuss the biggest and most important ones. It's not always easy being a teenager. While many adults are of the view that teenagers have it easy, it's far from the truth. An adult might have stability in their life with a job or a purpose. But it's a little difficult for teens like yourself to find their purpose. It's more like trying to find a needle in a haystack. The pressure of school, friends, extracurriculars, and family all collide while your body is growing. Not to mention, your hormones are off the charts. It's almost as if the world is leaning too much upon your shoulders.

Stress does not have an age limit. We often assume that just because teens have the luxury of staying at home and not worrying about the bills, they have fewer things to stress about.

You know what? That is far from the truth.

So, what causes all of this apprehension? Stress!

There are many possible triggers for anxiety and depression in teenagers. These include:

Trauma

Teenagers with a history of trauma—such as sexual abuse, violence, or involvement in an accident may be more likely to experience anxiety and depression (Klein, 2021). Trauma further translates into PTSD, which is one of the main triggers of stress and anxiety. For example, a teen who was in a car crash experienced some serious injuries, and their friends were traumatized by it. The traumatic event leads to stress, anxiety, and flashbacks of the accident, affecting their ability to cope with daily life and causing them immense emotional strain.

Environment

A teenager's social, school, and home environments can have an impact on their mental health. Difficulties such as abuse and neglect, divorce in the family, being bullied, poverty, learning disabilities, and struggling to fit in may all contribute to depression and anxiety. Besides, these stressors have a long-term effect on the teen's mind (Klein, 2021). For example, a high-pressure academic environment will trigger stress. The constant pressure to excel in exams, maintain a perfect GPA, and meet parental or societal expectations can overwhelm teenagers. They may experience stress-related symptoms like anxiety, sleep disturbances, and burnout due to the demanding and competitive environment.

Differences in the Brain

It's obvious that we are all made differently. But did you know that our minds age us? Yes, a teenage brain is structurally different from an adult brain. The young mind is more prone to sudden triggers. For example, after experiencing a tragic death in the family, a 14-year-old boy would process it differently from his 30-year-old father. In technical terms, changes in teenagers' brain circuits that are involved in responses to danger and rewards can increase stress levels. Teenagers with depression and anxiety may also have different levels of neurotransmitters—such as dopamine, serotonin, and norepinephrine—in their brains. These affect the regulation of moods and behavior.

Substance Misuse

Drug and alcohol misuse may affect teenagers' moods and lead to depression. They may turn to these substances to self-medicate their emotions (Klein, 2021). The misuse of alcohol or any other drug can lead to stressful experiences. For example, a teen who started experimenting with alcohol at social gatherings to fit in with their peers can become dependent on it to cope with stressors in their lives. They can experience heightened stress due to the pressure of hiding their addiction, the fear of getting caught, and the emotional toll it takes on their relationships and overall well-being. The cycle of substance abuse exacerbates their stress levels, leading to a vicious and harmful pattern in their lives.

Stresses of Puberty

Puberty can cause hormonal changes in teenagers that influence their mood, and this causes stress within them. It's a normal and common trigger. For example, Alex has started growing body hair, which makes him cover his whole body even when it's boiling outside. He feels like an outcast. However, it's important to remember that he is not alone and that everyone goes through puberty (Klein, 2021). Puberty can trigger stress in teenagers through the experience of body image concerns. Consider a teenage girl named Amy, who is going through various physical changes during puberty. As her body develops, she may feel self-conscious about these changes, comparing herself to societal beauty standards and her peers. The pressure to conform to certain ideals and the fear of being judged or teased can lead to heightened stress and negatively impact Amy's self-esteem and body confidence during this transitional period.

Negative Thought Patterns

Depression and anxiety in teenagers may be linked to negative thought patterns. If teenagers have regular exposure to negative thinking, often from their parents, they may also develop a negative worldview (Klein, 2021). Parents have a significant impact on how their children perceive the world; therefore, throughout DBT, teens are suggested to rethink any of their beliefs that may be biased.

World Events

Teenagers like yourself are alarmed by school shootings, terrorist attacks, and natural disasters. Teenagers are equally stressed out by these events. Assuming you have a smartphone or laptop, then you have access to the 24-hour news cycle, and after hearing about terrifying domestic and international news, you might start to worry for your own safety and the safety of your loved ones (Asamoah, 2020). For example, after a high-profile terrorist attack occurs in a nearby city, 15-year-old Sarah, a high school student, becomes deeply affected by the news and the media coverage surrounding the incident. The attack was widely reported, and discussions about it spread throughout her school and community. She becomes increasingly fearful for her safety, both at school and in public places. She starts to worry about the possibility of a similar attack happening in her own city or school. The attack she heard about on the news results in Sarah dealing with chronic stress and paranoia.

While the above list is not comprehensive, it does highlight the most common triggers of stress in teenagers. I imagine you have been affected by many of them yourself. So, now that you are aware of what stress is and its causes, let's move on to how DBT can really aid you in dealing with stress.

DBT to the Rescue

I really hope you will continue reading and learn how to utilize DBT skills to improve your life. As you know, DBT combines elements of cognitive-behavioral therapy with mindfulness practices, emphasizing skills training and acceptance-based strategies. We are about to jump into the four major tenets or parts of DBT, and you will see how, by implementing these skills into your life, you can minimize your stress levels and harmonize your mind and body. I will briefly mention each of the four parts here for you as a preview. The next chapters will explore them thoroughly and provide you with exercises to practice them.

Mindfulness

DBT incorporates mindfulness exercises that promote present-moment awareness and non-judgmental acceptance.

Engaging in mindfulness practices can help you reduce stress by cultivating a greater sense of calm, grounding, and a non-reactive attitude toward stressful thoughts and emotions. You can engage in meditation and active acceptance to promote calmness and reduce stress.

Distress Tolerance

The second tenet of DBT is distress tolerance. DBT teaches techniques to tolerate distressing situations without resorting to unhealthy coping mechanisms. It helps you develop skills to endure distress, manage crises, and navigate through challenging moments without becoming overwhelmed by stress. Whenever you feel distressed, engage in relaxation activities such as taking a warm bath or listening to soothing music. You can also engage in hobbies that make you feel relaxed and happy.

Emotion Regulation

The third tenet of DBT is emotional regulation. It provides you with skills to identify and regulate your emotions effectively. This includes techniques for managing intense emotions, reducing emotional reactivity, and increasing emotional resilience. By learning to regulate emotions, you can better cope with stressors. For example, you learn to recognize and label specific emotions such as anger, anxiety, and stress. Practicing deep breathing exercises, progressive muscle relaxation, and guided imagery can help calm the body and reduce stress.

Interpersonal Effectiveness

The fourth tenet of DBT is interpersonal effectiveness. DBT focuses on improving interpersonal skills such as effective communication, assertiveness, and setting healthy boundaries. Strengthening these skills can help individuals manage interpersonal stressors and enhance their relationships, reducing overall stress levels. This includes learning assertiveness skills and practicing "I" statements that can help you express your needs and boundaries clearly, reducing conflict and stress in your relationships.

This is merely a very brief preview of the four tenets of DBT and what they have to offer you. Each of them will be discussed in depth in their own chapters.

Final Words ...

In a nutshell, stress is a part of life. It's important to remember that you are not alone in your life and struggle. The signs of stress can often be confused with normal mood swings of teens, but it's imperative that you stay on the lookout for any extreme outbursts or irritation. It is very common for people your age to feel stress as the result of everyday life events as well as from triggers such as trauma, academic pressure, life-changing events, toxic family dynamics, etc. The biggest thing I want you to remember and hold onto is that the skills you are about to learn in the following pages and chapters can and will help you. DBT really does work, and you really can do this!

So, how do you apply the principles of DBT to reduce and minimize stress, anxiety, and depression? Let's take this step by step. The first step in the method of DBT is ...? Can you guess it? It has something to do with acceptance and non-judgment. If not, keep on reading.

CHAPTER 3:

THE ART OF NOW: LIVING IN THE MOMENT

"Mindfulness isn't difficult, we just need to remember to do it."

- Sharon Salzberg

So, if you haven't guessed it, mindfulness is the first core skill of DBT.

Mindfulness is an incredible and powerful skill, and guess what? You've got what it takes to master it! Just like any other skill, it can be learned and honed. All you need to do is embrace the learning process and make a commitment to practice it regularly. The more you engage in mindfulness, the smoother it gets and the more proficient you become. So, remember, practice makes perfect—and it's true for mindfulness too! You've got this!

I know we all want to eradicate our problems once and for all, but that's far from the truth. You cannot rely on a single technique to rid yourself of stress and anxiety.

You've likely come across the buzz about mindfulness and meditation, especially with its rise on TikTok and social media (Geall, n.d.). Celebrities and regular folks alike sing its praises, crediting the practice with life-changing effects. But what does it really mean?

At its core, mindfulness is all about nurturing a non-judgmental awareness of the present moment. It's about fully embracing the here and now and accepting it without attaching any judgments to it. By doing so, you can observe your thoughts, feelings, and behaviors without getting caught up in self-criticism or invalidation, which often leads to ongoing emotional struggles. Doing this allows you to observe your thoughts, feelings, and behaviors without engaging in self-criticism or invalidation, which often leads to ongoing emotional upheaval. It's like stepping into a space of calm and clarity where you can better understand yourself and the world around you. And believe me, that kind of self-awareness can truly be a game-changer!

Mindfulness involves being fully present in the moment and acknowledging our thoughts, emotions, and experiences without judgment. It's about observing and accepting whatever arises within us, whether positive or negative, without trying to change or suppress it. Do you remember Linehan's quote, "The path to healing begins with acceptance ...?" Mindfulness and acceptance are intertwined.

When you practice mindfulness, you learn to embrace your feelings and experiences as they are without attaching labels of good or bad. This non-judgmental acceptance allows you to create a compassionate space for yourself, fostering self-compassion and understanding. So, to exercise mindfulness, you have to accept however you are feeling without any judgment.

In the hustle and bustle of life, we often get caught up in evaluating our thoughts and emotions, categorizing them as desirable or undesirable. But mindfulness teaches us to let go of these judgments, liberating us from unnecessary stress and self-criticism (Geall, n.d.).

By accepting our feelings without judgment, we begin to cultivate a deeper connection with ourselves and the world around us. This newfound clarity enables us to respond to challenges and difficulties with more resilience and wisdom. We become less reactive and more open to experiencing life with curiosity and acceptance.

To give you a glimpse of how mindfulness and acceptance go hand in hand, let's look at how the connection between mindfulness and acceptance plays a central role in promoting emotional well-being and resilience. Mindfulness, a core component of DBT, involves being fully present in the moment and observing thoughts and emotions with openness and non-judgment.

You already know that DBT encourages individuals to practice mindful acceptance of their feelings and experiences without assigning value judgments. It emphasizes embracing all emotions, whether positive or negative, as valid and understandable responses to life's challenges. In DBT, mindfulness exercises, such as "Wise Mind," will help you develop the ability to identify and accept your emotions without being overwhelmed or controlled by them. Acceptance does not mean resignation or passivity; rather, it empowers you to acknowledge your emotions, assess situations objectively, and respond thoughtfully.

Through the integration of mindfulness and acceptance, DBT equips individuals with practical tools to manage stress, regulate emotions, and navigate life's challenges skillfully. By cultivating a deeper understanding and acceptance of yourself, you can build emotional resilience and cope with life's uncertainties more effectively.

So, why is mindfulness a part of DBT?

Well, mindfulness plays a vital role in DBT. It allows you to manage your emotions, cope with stress and anxiety, and create a satisfying and rewarding life.

Lauren is a typical teenager with a busy school life that often overwhelms her due to academic pressure. About a year ago, she started using social media, and since then, she has begun to feel that her life pales in comparison to everyone else's. On TikTok, she sees people with amazing hair and cool clothes, making it seem like they have it all—a great house, super cool friends, and fantastic clothes. Lauren finds herself constantly comparing herself to these people, feeling inadequate and "less than" them in terms of coolness, intelligence, and beauty. As a result, she has fallen into a state of depression and overwhelming emotions. Her increasing anger is causing tension with her friends and family, who are becoming fed up with her outbursts. She's at a loss for what to do and feels like everything is spiraling out of control.

Later that month, she received a diagnosis of OCD and began attending therapy sessions regularly. The therapist prescribed antidepressants and suggested she give meditation a try to help cope with the wide range of changes she was experiencing. Desperate for some relief, Lauren attempted meditation a couple of times over the course of a few weeks but quickly grew frustrated. She thought it didn't work at all and believed that all those people on social media who were raving about it were just exaggerating. Unfortunately, Lauren gave up on meditation and didn't commit to practicing it seriously (Geall, n.d.).

However, everything changed with the onset of the coronavirus pandemic. The weight of this global event crashed into her life, as it did for everyone else. Much like everyone else, she felt the familiar grip of anxiety growing and increasing in her life, and this time with more force.

After this realization, she decided to give mindfulness meditation another shot. I mean, why not? With plenty of free time stuck at home, she approached it with a more relaxed mindset, not expecting it to be a magical cure for her mental health issues or to eliminate anxiety forever. Instead, she wondered if mindfulness meditation could help her gain better control over her thoughts and emotions. So, she made a firm commitment to incorporate meditation into her daily routine.

Lauren became serious and disciplined about it. Every day, without fail, she set aside 20 minutes for meditation. No matter her mood—good, bad, angry, anxious, or relatively okay— she stuck to it. There was no judgment or criticism of herself or how the meditation session went; she simply accepted it and continued the practice. Day after day, week after week, she persevered with her daily meditation sessions.

Eventually, Lauren realized that she felt calmer and more at peace with who she was and what she did. The restlessness she felt throughout her day almost faded away. Meditation allowed her to tap into the sense of calmness that she longed for, and it created a positive ambiance around herself that enabled her to be mindful of the things she did throughout her day and how she lived her life. In fact, her brother also mentioned how she became a lot more laid back and chill, which was a compliment to her! The thing that worked in her favor was identifying her emotions and labeling them. This not only helped her understand the root cause of what she felt and why she felt it but also how she could heal that specific source of discomfort (Geall, n.d.).

PSA: Later in this chapter, I have activities planned for you that allow you to practice meditation, so let's go!

What Is Mindfulness?

So, mindfulness is all about being fully present in the moment and without any judgment or getting caught up in thoughts about the past or worries about the future. Bill Keane puts it perfectly: "'Yesterday is history, tomorrow is a mystery, today is a gift of God, which is why we call it the present." Mindfulness forces you to step out of the rush that exists within society and reconnect with yourself (Crumpler et al., 2022).

Mindfulness is about stopping your mind from running away from you, returning to the past, and reliving an event that went wrong over and over again. It is about stopping your mind from running ahead of yourself and obsessing over how you are going to fail at some task looming in the future. It is about keeping your mind in the present moment, being mindful of that moment, and living in your present moment.

It's about tuning into your senses and really noticing things like your breath and the sensations in your body. It's like embracing the present moment and being "in the now."

If you're dealing with thoughts that make you feel really uneasy or uncomfortable, starting a mindfulness practice could be a great way to bring yourself back to the present moment. It can help you let go of stress and find some peace. Meditation is the foundational premise of mindfulness. It is promoted in religions, cultures, and regions as a source of wisdom, self-awareness, and harmony, all for the right reasons (Crumpler et al., 2022).

But how?

That's a good question.

Mindfulness allows you to step back from your thoughts and worries and focus on the present moment. By practicing mindfulness, you can develop awareness of your stress triggers and learn to respond to them in a more calm and balanced manner. Most importantly, it helps you refocus and divide your attention according to your priorities. Now that's interesting, right?

Let's take an example. You have a test in three days for which you have not studied at all. You are on the verge of a mental breakdown, spiraling with stress and having frequent outbursts. You find yourself in a tricky situation. What do you do?

Take a step back.

Breathe.

Sit down for five minutes and clear your mind.

When preparing for tests, anxiety can be overwhelming. Mindfulness allows you to acknowledge and observe your anxiety without judgment, creating space between you and your anxious thoughts. When the space is created, use it to prioritize your strengths of the subject and focus on the weaknesses so that you can bridge the gap of lost time.

By practicing mindfulness, you can develop a calmer and more balanced mindset, which can help alleviate exam-related stress. Besides, engaging in mindfulness exercises, such as deep breathing or progressive muscle relaxation, can activate your body's relaxation response.

Deep breathing exercises are a simple yet powerful way to reduce stress, calm the mind, and promote relaxation. Let me walk you through a step-by-step guide to practicing deep breathing:

1. Find a Comfortable Position

Start by finding a quiet and comfortable place to sit or lie down. You can also choose to stand if that feels more natural for you.

2. Straighten Your Posture

Sit or stand up straight with your shoulders relaxed. Place your hands on your abdomen, just below your ribcage, to feel the movement of your breath.

3. Inhale Slowly

Take a slow and deep breath in through your nose. As you breathe in, feel your abdomen expand. Imagine you are filling up a balloon in your belly with each breath. Pause for a moment at the top of your inhale without straining. Allow yourself to fully experience the sensation of having a lungful of air.

4. Exhale Gradually

Slowly exhale through your mouth or nose, whichever feels more comfortable. As you breathe out, feel your abdomen gently contract and release the air (Crumpler et al., 2022).

5. Repeat the Process

Continue this deep breathing pattern for a few minutes, focusing on the sensation of your breath entering and leaving your body. Let go of any tension or distractions as you concentrate on the rhythm of your breath (Crumpler et al., 2022).

Deep breathing exercises are a simple yet effective way to ground yourself in the present moment and find inner calmness. Practicing this technique regularly can help reduce stress, lower anxiety levels, and promote overall well-being. Remember, you can do deep breathing exercises anytime and anywhere, making them a valuable tool for managing stress and finding balance in your daily life.

Another useful skill in practicing mindfulness is progressive muscle relaxation (PMR). It is a relaxation technique that involves tensing and relaxing different muscle groups to release tension and promote a sense of calm. Here's a step-by-step guide on how to do it:

1. Find a Quiet Space

Begin by finding a quiet and comfortable space where you can sit or lie down. Remove any distractions and ensure you have enough privacy to fully focus on the exercise.

2. Get Comfortable

Sit or lie in a relaxed position with your eyes closed. Take a few deep breaths to settle into the present moment and clear your mind.

3. Start with Your Hands

Begin by focusing on your hands. Clench your fists tightly and hold the tension for about 5 to 10 seconds. Pay attention to the sensations of tightness in your hands (Crumpler et al., 2022).

4. Release the Tension

After holding the tension, slowly release your fists and let your hands relax completely. Pay attention to the feeling of relaxation spreading through your hands (Crumpler et al., 2022).

5. Move to Your Forearms

Gradually shift your focus to your forearms. Tense the muscles in your forearms by flexing them and holding for 5 to 10 seconds.

6. Release and Relax

Let go of the tension in your forearms and allow them to completely relax. Feel the warmth and comfort as the tension fades away.

7. Work through Your Body

Continue this process of tensing and relaxing different muscle groups throughout your body. Progressively move through your upper arms, shoulders, neck, jaw, face, chest, abdomen, lower back, hips, thighs, calves, and feet.

8. Take Your Time

Spend about 5 to 10 seconds tensing each muscle group and then around 20 to 30 seconds fully relaxing them. Take your time to focus on each muscle group and the contrast between tension and relaxation (Crumpler et al., 2022).

You can practice PMR daily, especially during times of heightened stress or before bedtime, to improve sleep quality and overall well-being.

Let's Talk about Meditation

You have undoubtedly heard about meditation. It is super popular with celebrities and is constantly being talked about on social media. But what exactly is it?

Let's get right into it. Meditation has a rich and unique history. It is a practice that's been around for centuries and has its roots in various cultures and traditions. It's a technique that helps you focus your mind and achieve a sense of inner peace and tranquility (Scott, 2022).

The history of meditation goes way back—like, really, way back! It's believed to have originated over 5,000 years ago in ancient India, where it was initially used as a spiritual practice to deepen one's connection with the divine. The ancient Indian scriptures, the Vedas, mention meditation as a means to attain higher states of consciousness and self-realization.

As time went on, meditation spread to other parts of the world, finding its way into Buddhist and Taoist practices in China, as well as becoming an essential part of various Eastern philosophies and religions (Scott, 2022).

In the West, meditation gained popularity in the mid-20th century, thanks to teachers like Maharishi Mahesh Yogi, who introduced transcendental meditation to the world. Since then, it has become increasingly recognized for its many benefits, from reducing stress and anxiety to improving focus and overall well-being (Cherry, 2022).

Today, meditation is practiced in various forms and styles across the globe. From mindfulness meditation, where you focus on the present moment, to loving-kindness meditation, where you cultivate feelings of compassion toward yourself and others, there are so many ways to explore this ancient practice.

Meditation is all about finding that quiet time to connect with yourself and discover a sense of inner peace. So, whether you're a seasoned meditator or new to the practice, there's no right or wrong way to do it. It's all about finding what works best for you and taking that journey toward a more centered and mindful life!

So, how often should you do it, and how should you do it?

Meditation is a wonderful practice that anyone can try, and it's surprisingly simple to get started. Here's how you can do it:

- **Find a Quiet Space:** Choose a quiet and comfortable spot where you won't be disturbed. You can sit on a cushion or chair with your back straight and your hands resting comfortably (Cherry, 2022).

- **Focus on Your Breath:** Close your eyes and take a few deep breaths to settle in. Pay attention to the sensation of your breath as you inhale and exhale. Let go of any thoughts or distractions.

- **Be Consistent:** The key to successful meditation is consistency. Try to practice daily, even if it's only for a few minutes. It's better to meditate for a short time regularly than for a long time sporadically (Cherry, 2022).

Remember, meditation is a skill that takes time to develop. Don't be hard on yourself if your mind wanders or if you find it challenging to stay focused at first, which is completely normal and expected. Be patient with yourself and keep going. Meditation is not about achieving immediate success or perfecting your practice. It's about the journey of self-discovery and finding moments of peace and clarity along the way.

Meditation can be a transformative practice, but like any skill, it requires discipline and patience. Some days, your mind might be more restless, and other days, you'll find deeper moments of stillness. The key is to continue showing up for yourself and making meditation a regular part of your life (Scott, 2022).

With time and dedication, you'll likely notice positive changes in your emotional well-being, focus, and overall outlook on life. So, remember, there's no right or wrong way to meditate, and every session is an opportunity to learn more about yourself and find moments of peace in the midst of our busy lives. Enjoy the journey!

Mindfulness & DBT

In DBT, mindfulness is emphasized and reinforced consistently throughout the treatment process. It serves as the foundation for each skill's training session because all other emotion regulation skills in DBT rely on the practice of mindfulness. However, despite its crucial role in DBT skills, the true purpose of DBT mindfulness, which is to decrease emotional sensitivity and facilitate emotional regulation, is frequently misunderstood (Bonfil, 2014).

In simpler words, what is mindfulness in DBT?

Although it may seem simple, many people spend only a small portion of their day mindfully engaged in their own lives. We often disconnect from our actual experiences and become absorbed in our thoughts about those experiences. This habitual engagement with our thoughts rather than with reality makes it easy to lose sight of what is truly happening to us and, consequently, how best to effectively handle our experiences.

You already know that DBT is a treatment that targets emotion dysregulation. Often, people get emotionally dysregulated by seemingly insignificant or trivial events, not because of the events themselves but by the judgments people have about the events. For example, you have a math test that you are unprepared for—so you spend the rest of the day after the test lamenting and engaging in negative self-talk: "I'll fail" or "I should have just stayed at home ..." "Why am I so bad at math?"

A mindful approach to this dilemma would be to approach the unpleasant task in the spirit of acceptance, willing to engage in it without engaging in a lot of judgments about it. The moment you notice a judgment, you turn your mind to a hobby, such as reading, for example. Every time your mind is deceived by a negative thought, divert it toward finishing another chapter of your favorite novel (Lee & Gottlieb, 2018). By fully engaging in the task and repeatedly turning the mind to it, there is little room for negative attributions. You may now even find it to be a calming, soothing activity. This is one way that mindfulness can help avert an emotional downward spiral.

Mindfully experiencing emotions involves observing them without attempting to control or suppress them. Instead, you simply notice and accept each aspect of the emotion as it arises. For example, you might become aware of a flushed face or a lump in your throat. This is where mindfulness comes in, as it allows you to accept these experiences unconditionally without clinging to them or pushing them away (Bonfil, 2014). You create a no-judgment zone for yourself.

It's like accepting that you can't argue with emotion because it serves a purpose. The paradoxical approach of mindfulness involves tolerating the emotion without resistance, which ultimately leads to less distressing and shorter-lasting emotional experiences. By giving permission for emotions to be present, they naturally run their course as transient, ever-changing sensations (Lee & Gottlieb, 2018).

Benefits of Mindfulness

Did you know that mindfulness has the capacity to slow down brain aging? It's like retinol, but instead of preventing skin aging, it supports cognitive functionality and ensures that our brain ages gracefully. Much like this, there are several other benefits of mindfulness. Here is a list of some of the most important benefits that mindfulness has to offer:

Reduced Depression

Depression is like a black hole; once stuck in it, you feel like you are falling deeper and deeper into it. Mindfulness combined with meditation is a powerful tool that can aid you in your healing journey. Mindfulness-based cognitive therapy (MBCT) is like a blend of compassionate support and practical tools. It weaves together cognitive-behavioral therapy (CBT) with mindfulness-based stress reduction (MBSR), creating an eight-week journey that unfolds through group sessions warmed by the embrace of mindfulness practices. So, when you embark on this journey, you'll not only find practices but also pathways to self-discovery. Meditation, body scans, and yoga form part of this nurturing space that encourages self-awareness and a kind embrace of your thoughts. It's one step closer to healing (Cho, 2022).

Emotional Regulation

Did you know that mindfulness can reshape your brain's response to emotion, creating a balance? Mindfulness helps you to recognize and navigate your emotions, a vital skill for your mental well-being. It also helps you deal with challenges in controlling emotions that often relate to conditions like depression and BPD. It also empowers teens to engage in better coping and enhancing relationships, setting them on the path of personal growth and healing (Cherry, 2022).

Lessen Anxiety & Stress

In 2016, a study highlighted that mindfulness is a readily accessible and cost-effective method for easing negative emotions, stress, and anxiety. In this age of increasing inflation and a crippling economy, it's important to make use of such valuable and inexpensive strategies to help you in your healing journey.

Enhance Memory

Have you ever wondered why you keep forgetting about your assignment deadlines? It's majorly because your older memories overshadow the newer ones. So, how does mindfulness help in this case?

A study from 2019 had participants engage in four weeks of mindfulness training or a creative writing course. Those who embraced mindfulness exhibited significant decreases in proactive interference, leading to better short-term memory (Cherry, 2022).

The benefits don't stop at performance alone; they extend to physical changes in the brain. Brain imaging revealed shifts in hippocampal volume among those who practiced mindfulness—a brain area essential for memory (Harvard Health, 2023).

So, these are some benefits that you will experience when adapting to mindfulness in your DBT journey. But, there is something significant that I want to redirect your attention toward. Do you remember that I mentioned the "WISE mind" activity at the beginning of this chapter?

DBT Activities

I will share three activities with you that will help you practice mindfulness, help you navigate your emotions better, and release any tension from your body.

Wise Mind

WISE mind is a famous extension of mindfulness in the DBT course. Naturally, humans operate in extremes, so we often operate from a place of pure reason or pure logic. When we are viewing the world through either lens, we miss out on the big picture. Viewing events and relationships purely with logic can come across as distant. Conversely, perceiving life solely through emotion can lead to a sense of chaos and disorder. In order to live the most effective and balanced lives possible, it is advantageous to learn how to integrate reason with emotion. This integration is "WISE mind."

So, what is the technique behind this tool?

DBT makes use of unique concepts that deal with the three states of mind, namely: reasonable, emotional, and wise. Think of the "reasonable mind" as the logic center, the "emotional mind" as the feelings zone, and the "wise mind" hanging out right in the middle.

What does each of these states represent?

Reasonable Mind

This is where we put on our logical thinking caps and focus on the hard facts and stuff we can actually see and observe. Have you ever felt a bit distant from a situation, like you're stepping back and looking at it from a logical perspective? That's the reasonable mind in action. It's like you're taking in the facts, making plans based purely on what you can see and know. It's all about that cool, rational thinking (Dialectical Behavior Therapy, 2020).

Emotional Mind

Have you felt like your emotions were so strong that thinking straight got a bit hazy? For example, have you ever been peer pressured into skipping class or bunking school? In that moment, regardless of the risky activity that your peers were pushing you into, you made an emotional decision and said yes. It's almost like the emotions can put a funhouse mirror spin on situations, making them look bigger or more intense even though they aren't. But it's okay because going through an emotional phase is normal and part of the healing journey.

Wise Mind

Wise mind is that sweet spot between reason and emotion—the perfect balance. It's like the "middle way." It's all about deep, intuitive thinking. It goes beyond just logic and relies on what your senses tell you. This super intuition comes from blending direct experience, quick understanding, and grasping the meaning of something without overthinking (Dialectical Behavior Therapy, 2020).

How you experience a wise mind might be different from others. For some, it's that calm voice inside that knows what's up. You might not always follow it, but it's there, quietly dropping wisdom. For others, it's like that "gut feeling" about what's the right move. And guess what? We all have a wise mind waiting to be explored! I have designed a cohesive WISE mind activity for you to practice. Again, always remember that in order to master this skill, you will have to be consistent with it.

Now you know that everyone possesses each of these states, but most people gravitate toward a specific one most of the time. Here is the gist of each of the states:

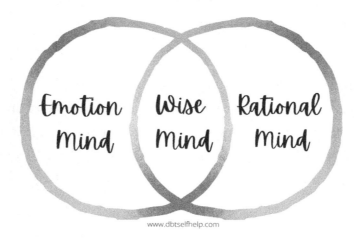

www.dbtselfhelp.com

The **emotional mind** is used when feelings control a person's thoughts and behavior. They might act impulsively with little regard for consequences.	The **wise mind** refers to a balance between the reasonable and emotional halves. They are able to recognize and respect their feelings, while responding to them in a rational manner.	A person uses their **reasonable mind** when they approach a situation intellectually. They plan and make decisions based on fact.

Describe an experience you've had with each of the three states of mind:

Emotional	
Wise	
Reasonable	

When you set out to hone your wise mind skills, try to integrate these practices into your daily routine (Dialectical Behavior Therapy, 2020).

- **Breathe Mindfully**

Get comfortable, breathe in and out, and focus on your breath filling and leaving your lungs. Shift your attention from the bottom to the top of each breath, right at your third eye.

- **Embrace Pauses**

While breathing mindfully, feel the "pause" after each inhale and exhale, like stillness between trapeze bars. Find that calm in the pauses at the breath's top and bottom.

- **Stone Flake Visualization**

Imagine sitting by a clear lake. Picture yourself as a stone flake floating on the water's surface. Slowly sink to the peaceful sandy lake bottom. Feel the tranquility there, your inner calm center (Mindfulness Therapy Associates, 2022).

Body Scan Meditation

This is the second activity that I want to introduce you to. Sometimes, you can be so caught up in your stress that you don't realize that the physical discomfort you're experiencing—such as headaches, back and shoulder pain, and tense muscles—is connected to your emotional state. Body scan meditation can help ease hidden tension. It's about tuning into your body, from toes to head, and acknowledging any discomfort. This isn't about vanishing pain but understanding it to handle it better. You're not alone in this journey to relief (Scott, 2021).

Here is a step-by-step guide on how you can incorporate body scan meditation into your daily life:

1. Get comfortable.

It's best to lie down, especially if you're doing a pre-sleep body scan meditation. If lying down isn't comfortable for you, sitting comfortably is also an excellent option. The key is to find what works best for you!

2. Take a few deep breaths.

Let your breathing slow down and start breathing from your belly instead of from your chest, letting your abdomen expand and contract with each breath. Try to focus on breathing from your belly (Scott, 2021).

3. Bring awareness to your feet.

Direct your focus to your feet. Gradually shift your attention downward. Notice sensations in your feet. If you feel pain, recognize it along with any thoughts or emotions, and breathe gently through it.

4.Breathe into the tension.

When you inhale, if you feel any discomfort, direct your focus there. Inhale into that tension and focus your attention on it. Imagine the tension escaping as you exhale, fading into the air.

5. Scan your entire body.

Keep up this routine for each body section, slowly progressing from your feet to your head. Tune into your tension and stress points. If you sense tightness, pain, or pressure, keep breathing into those feelings. This lets you unwind and builds awareness for future relief (Scott, 2021).

Describe Your Emotions

When you are able to identify and label your emotions for what they really are, you are able to control them in the future. For example, when you feel sad, instead of mislabeling it as anger, identify the root cause of it. This activity will help you understand your emotions and label them correctly so that you are able to deal with them accordingly (DBT Self Help, n.d.). Complete the table below (bonus: you can reuse this table as many times as you like):

A List of Emotions

Go beyond the obvious to identify exactly what you're feeling.

Angry	Sad	Anxious	Hurt	Embarrassed	Happy
Grumpy	Disappointed	Afraid	Jealous	Isolated	Thankful
Frustrated	Mournful	Stressed	Betrayed	Self-conscious	Trusting
Annoyed	Regretful	Vulnerable	Isolated	Lonely	Comfortable
Defensive	Depressed	Confused	Shocked	Inferior	Content
Spiteful	Paralyzed	Bewildered	Deprived	Guilty	Excited
Impatient	Pessimistic	Skeptical	Victimized	Ashamed	Relaxed
Disgusted	Tearful	Worried	Aggrieved	Repugnant	Relieved
Offended	Dismayed	Cautious	Tormented	Pathetic	Elated
Irritated	Disillusioned	Nervous	Abandoned	Confused	Confident

SOURCE SUSAN DAVID   © HBR.ORG

Pick an emotion from the list above.	
Draw a picture of your emotion.	
Write an action suitable to your emotion.	
Describe the Intensity of your emotion.	
Write your thoughts arising from your emotions.	

Final Words ...

So, you are now aware of the first tenant of DBT, which is mindfulness. By now, you must have understood that you are not alone in how you feel. Emotions can be overwhelming, and stress can be exhausting; therefore, it is always important to engage in activities that revive peace in your life.

Mindfulness not only helps you cope with the stressful factors of your life, but it also aims to promote calmness during an overwhelming moment. Engaging in mindful activities such as wise mind and emotion labeling can help you regain momentum back into your life and also ensure that you make informed decisions for yourself. I encourage you to pick out one activity and use it religiously in your daily life.

Speaking of emotions, DBT targets this particular aspect as a whole in its journey. If you are struggling with disrupted emotional patterns, then this is for you—flip the page and find out!

CHAPTER 4:

INTERNAL ROLLER COASTER: CALMING THE CHAOS

"In the midst of movement and chaos, keep stillness inside of you."

- Deepak Chopra

Our life is a vast ocean of emotions, where every wave crashes onto our shores with its own distinct intensity and impact. As we sail through this grand journey of existence, we often find ourselves entangled in the unpredictable currents of our feelings, occasionally swept away by their sheer power. It's in these very moments of emotional whirlwinds that we ache for a lifeline—a beacon to steer us through the tempest with unyielding strength and a touch of elegance (Psychology Today, 2021).

Have you ever felt like crying all the time, whether it's at work, behind the wheel, sprawled out on the couch, or even during a shower? If you feel this way, don't worry; you are not alone. Alex sails in the same boat of emotional warfare.

He once cried at the thought of his eight-month-old puppy growing up. Now, who doesn't cry when their little puppy is growing up? That emotional episode was expected. Another time, he cried because his college math professor unfairly gave his classmate a higher grade than him. And don't even get started on that unforgettable King Viserys scene from the *House of the Dragon* series—apparently, stag-stabbing isn't the norm, but it hit Alex right in the feels, and his eyes welled up with tears. Let's be honest; we all cried a little when this happened (Andrews, 2022).

However, before you start thinking sensitivity is a weakness, that's far from the truth—it's a superpower, and Alex is winning. It's incredible how he can feel everything so deeply. But this might make you wonder—how does Alex keep these emotions from overwhelming him? Well, he has got a weekly routine—a scheduled cry session—and trust me, it's a game-changer.

Here's how this works:

Every week, Alex carves out a chunk of time in his schedule and calls it "The Great Cry." It's an appointment he makes with himself, dedicated solely to letting those emotions flow. Sometimes, it's all kicked off with a heart-wrenching movie like *About Time*. Other times, the tears simply start rolling, and no movie cues are required (Andrews, 2022).

Physically, it's as if Alex is cleansing his system of all the built-up emotional weight. During these sessions, he is able to really connect with his emotions and understand where they are stemming from. Mentally, it's like he is sorting through doubts, fears, and whatever life tosses his way—but in a healthy, systematic manner. During these sessions, it's like a dam bursts open, and Alex lets out all those bottled-up feelings. It's like an emotional waterfall, with each emotion leading to the next, creating a cascade of release. It all works out in his favor because he is able to regulate his emotions effectively.

But here's the fascinating part: science backs up this crying ritual. Turns out, crying isn't just about tears; it's a way to unload all that emotional baggage that's been stored up. It's like hitting a reset button on these feelings. Have you ever felt like, after a crying session, you feel a lot better than you expected? It's because you are able to unload pent-up, untapped emotions that have been ignored for some time (Andrews, 2022).

But for Alex, it's more than that. These sessions help him regain control over his emotions. Before, tears had a tendency to pop up at the most unexpected moments—like when he was asked for extra ranch at McDonald's and got an eye-roll in response. Stress and anxiety used to trigger tears like a switch. According to a licensed professional counselor, it's all about unloading that tension that builds up. Crying is a release valve for all that emotional pressure.

Of course, it's important to note that this isn't about suppressing tears. If Alex feels like crying, he doesn't shy away from it. This is about creating a designated space to process his emotions. Sure, he might still have spontaneous teary moments outside these sessions—he's only human, after all. However, his weekly cry ritual helps him work through the emotions that might otherwise pile up (Andrews, 2022).

And each time, he came out of the session feeling a bit lighter and a bit more centered. But here's the thing—this method might not work the same for everyone, and that's totally okay. It's about discovering your own personal release valve, whether it's yoga, meditation, or any other form of self-care that resonates.

So, do you sometimes feel like your emotions are overflowing and that there is nothing you can do about it?

Sometimes, life is burdensome, and we stumble because of the pressure and anxiety. Our emotions get disrupted, and we have meltdowns. But that's all a part of life. As a teen, you are often thrust into situations that might be overwhelming, such as having a test on the same day as your basketball game or your family member getting into an accident while you have an interview with your dream college. Whether you are a freshman, sophomore, or college student, stress and emotional instability will accompany you everywhere. So, how do you deal with it? We have talked about how you can deal with stress in the previous chapters, but when it comes to emotional dysregulation, it's important to understand the causes, identify the roots, and then give yourself ample space to recover from the burden.

When teens opt for DBT, emotional regulation is the second tenant in that process. This is where professionals help you understand how you can cope with emotions that tamper with your well-being. For you to understand the complete scope of your emotional range, you'll have to recognize what emotional regulation is and why it's important.

What Is Emotional Regulation?

Emotional regulation is the ability to exert control over your own emotional state. For example, you control your anger or anxiety, conceal obvious symptoms of sadness or fear, or focus on reasons to be cheerful or happy. When your emotions are regulated, you feel at ease.

Have you ever felt like your life is chaotic and you cannot get a hold of your emotions?

If you're someone who sometimes feels like your emotions are all over the place, you're not alone. Imagine your feelings as these super intense waves that just keep coming and changing—kind of like a roller coaster ride for your emotions!

Emotional regulation is like having a superpower over your own feelings. It's about doing things to manage how you're feeling. Like, when a tough situation makes you mad or super anxious, you might take a step back and think about it in a different way to calm down. Or maybe you've learned how to hide when you're sad or scared on the outside, even if you're feeling that way inside. Sometimes, you might even try to focus on things that make you happy or peaceful to balance things out. It's all about having control over how you feel and reacting in a way that helps you handle things better (Psychology Today, 2021).

Primary & Secondary Emotions

Did you know that our emotions are divided into secondary and primary emotions?

The name gives it away for primary emotions. They are the first thing we feel—the immediate rush of anger or excitement; however, the secondary emotions are what you should be on the lookout for!

Think of the secondary emotion as the one that comes after the first one, kind of like a follow-up. Let's say you get super angry about something, and then right after that, you start feeling ashamed. So, in this case, anger is the first emotion, and shame is the second one—like it's following along (Psychology Today, 2021).

When you are trying to regulate your emotions, it's important to figure out which emotions are which. It's like being a detective for your feelings! Because, to handle an emotion and deal with it, you've got to get to the heart of the matter—that's the primary emotion.

Surprisingly, sometimes, the second emotion can actually be the same as the first one. Like, you could get angry because you're already angry, or you might feel down because you're already feeling down.

In those cases, your secondary and primary emotions are the same.

Have you ever felt like something triggered your anger while you were upset? For example, you were upset with your sister because she wore your favorite shirt to school, and later, you got angry at your friend for using your makeup. In this case, your primary and secondary emotions are both negative. Therefore, it's important to catch this synonymity and cohesiveness between your emotions.

Here's a tip: Keep an eye out for shame, especially as a secondary emotion. For instance, if you snapped in anger, you might feel ashamed afterward. So, it's like there's a lot going on under the surface of our feelings, and figuring it out helps us understand ourselves better (Chowdhury & Smith, 2019).

What are some of the common ways you respond to your emotions?

What do you do when you get angry?

It's normal to feel like the world is against you when you are emotionally distressed. You might even feel like no one is on your side or that everyone is plotting against you, but that is far from the truth. What you are feeling right now is your response to emotional distress and should not take a toll on your mental health.

Some of the common ways people process emotions include feeling jittery when they're worried about something or even feeling scared about what might happen. Anger and frustration lead to intense reactions or outbursts, like throwing things or stomping away from the people you love. Sometimes, we feel like we've done something wrong or let someone down, and that's guilt kicking in, but this is different from shame because that makes you hide in your room or avoid people. Similarly, when things get too intense, you might feel emotionally numb, like you're not feeling anything at all, or you might feel overwhelmed when emotions pile up. You might feel like you can't handle it all. Our responses to emotions play a large role in how we address the dysregulation in our emotional capacity and simultaneously self-regulate (Chowdhury & Smith, 2019).

Importance of Emotional Regulation

Let me rephrase the heading—why is emotional self-regulation important?

Imagine emotions like the buttons on a control panel, and you're the one holding the remote; you are in control of your emotions. Emotional self-regulation is the remote that lets you manage those buttons wisely.

Imagine you are in a room with your relatives, and one of them mentions an incident that hurt the entire family last year. Midway through the conversation, suddenly, your emotions start bubbling up inside you. Now, here's where it gets interesting. If you're a pro at emotional self-regulation, you've got this pause button. It's like hitting the brakes on your own feelings, giving you space to actually listen to what the other person is saying. It's not just about you; it's about understanding where they're coming from, too. Aside from hurtful memories, self-regulation of emotions also comes into play when life throws you a curveball. This helps when you see disappointment knocking on your door. Instead of flipping out, emotional self-regulation helps you keep your cool and think things through rationally. It's like having your own emotional shield against the unexpected.

Have you ever seen a kid who tosses things around or has tantrums?

Well, they're still figuring out how to manage those buttons. And guess what? It's not just kids—even teenagers and young adults can struggle with it. If you can't tame those emotions, it might lead to not-so-great ways of dealing with stuff, like using substances or making poor choices. Mastering emotional self-regulation is like unlocking a secret level. It helps you become the master of conflict resolution, where even heated debates can end in calm solutions. And here's the thing—it doesn't mean you're banishing feelings like anger, sadness, or disappointment. Nope, they're still part of the game. Emotional self-regulation is more like a strategy guide for dealing with them. It stops you from going all out and reacting impulsively, especially when things are totally out of your hands.

Emotional Regulation & DBT

In DBT, emotional regulation plays a huge role in labeling and understanding emotions. It serves as the heart of the whole treatment process. As you already know, DBT can help you understand your emotions, manage them properly, and live a healthier life. And that's where emotion regulation comes into play (DBT Self Help, 2020).

Think of it as a toolbox full of strategies. Imagine you have this big, cool toolbox, and inside, you've got tools to handle different emotions—like a wrench for anger, a screwdriver for sadness, and so on. Emotion regulation in DBT gives you these tools, so when you're feeling overwhelmed, you're not left empty-handed. Our emotions can lead to increasingly destructive actions if not regulated properly.

This is why mastering the art of emotion regulation is at the heart of DBT. But let's clear something up right away—it's not about saying your feelings aren't real or don't matter. They're valid, they matter, and they're just a natural part of being human. However, sometimes, emotions can feel like a wild roller coaster that you didn't sign up for. They can cause a lot of pain and might even make you feel like you're not in charge anymore. So, it's important to learn how you can manage them. It's like having a toolkit to handle these ups and downs.

It starts with acknowledging your emotions and giving them a nod of recognition. Then it's about saying, "Hey, it's okay to feel this way." It's like giving yourself permission to feel without judging yourself for it. DBT breaks it down into steps. You learn to recognize and name your emotions, which is like figuring out which tool you need from your emotional toolbox. Then, you learn strategies to manage those feelings—things like mindfulness to stay present, distress tolerance to handle tough situations, and interpersonal effectiveness to communicate better. As you practice these skills, you're building up this amazing power to handle your emotions like a pro. It's not about being perfect—everyone has ups and downs—but it's about having the tools to ride the emotional roller coaster with strength and confidence (DBT Self Help, 2020).

Here is how you can use DBT and incorporate emotional regulating practices in your daily life:

Identifying Emotions

This is like putting a name to what you're feeling. Sometimes, emotions can be a jumble, but DBT helps you break them down and figure out what's going on inside.

Understanding Emotions

Once you know what you're feeling, you dig deeper. What triggered that emotion? How intense is it? Understanding the "why" behind your emotions can help you manage them better (Juby, 2022).

Accepting Emotions

This is a biggie. It's about letting yourself feel what you're feeling without judgment. Remember, emotions are totally okay, even the negative ones.

Changing Emotions

Here's where you learn to tweak those intense emotions. DBT gives you strategies to balance things out. Think of it like adjusting the volume on a radio—you're not turning it off, just finding the right level.

Building Positive Experiences

This is all about adding things into your life that make you feel good. It's like refueling your emotional tank with positivity.

Managing Crises

Life can throw curveballs, right? DBT helps you develop skills to handle those emotional storms without losing your balance (Juby, 2022).

Mindfulness

This is like your secret weapon. It's about staying present in the moment, which can help you deal with emotions as they come instead of getting overwhelmed.

Distress Tolerance

Sometimes situations get tough, and it's like you're in a pressure cooker. DBT gives you tools to tolerate that distress and get through it.

Interpersonal Effectiveness

This is all about communication. Learning how to express your needs and understand others can make a huge difference in managing your emotions.

Self-Validation

Think of this as giving yourself a pat on the back. You're acknowledging your feelings and being kind to yourself, even when things get tough.

Self-Soothing

Just like you might comfort a friend, DBT teaches you how to comfort yourself when emotions run high.

Problem-Solving

Sometimes, there are things you can change to make things better. DBT helps you find solutions to the things that trigger your intense emotions. Hence, by allowing your emotions to be validated and completely understood, DBT helps you regulate them effectively.

While these are the basic steps, there are some specific activities that you refer to when trying to regulate your emotions (Juby, 2022).

DBT Activities

I will share three activities with you that will help you practice emotional regulation, help you understand your emotions, and navigate through them better.

Balancing Emotional Urges

Instructions

Step 1
What Are Opposites?

First, we have to get familiar with what the opposites of the usual emotional urges are. Let's take four emotions into consideration since they have the most potential to lead to ineffective behaviors: anger, sadness, anxiety, and shame. We won't focus on positive emotions because they usually lead to positive behaviors, such as approaching others and being effective and motivated. In the table below, we will identify the emotion, the urge it is inciting, and what can be the positive opposite of it (Koonce, 2018):

Emotion	Urge	Opposite Urge
Anger	To verbally or physically attack someone	Being polite, more gentle, or nice
Anxiety/fear	To avoid the anxiety-provoking situation	To remain in the anxiety-provoking situation
Sadness	To isolate yourself from others	To seek support and socialize
Shame	To hide from people or to avoid them	To approach others and share your thoughts (if appropriate)

Step 2
Emotion and Effectiveness of the Emotional Urge

Once you are aware of opposite emotional responses, follow these two steps: First, when overwhelmed by emotions, identify your feelings. Then, assess if expressing natural impulses is suitable. If you are angry, instead of reacting to your impulses and having an outburst, try to distance yourself from the main trigger.

Step 3
Act Opposite

The concept of countering emotional urges involves adopting opposing actions until the emotion shifts or lessens. Initially, this might feel unnatural. You have to recognize the urge to hide when ashamed or avoid anxiety-inducing situations that arise from feelings, but feelings aren't always reliable guides. They're transient and programmed responses.

Lastly, repeat the whole process again. Use the table below as your personal tablet for creating opposite emotional reactions to negative feelings (Koonce, 2018):

Situation	
Emotion and effectiveness of emotional urge	
Acting the opposite way	
Repeat	

Self-Validation

Instructions

Level 1

Step 1
Acknowledging

Recognize your current emotion without judgment. Name what you're feeling, like "I feel sad," avoiding self-deprecating spirals like "I'm always down, so weak and unworthy." Just acknowledge the emotion: "I feel sad."

Step 2
Allowing

This step centers on accepting all emotions. You can permit your feelings in any situation, even when intense. Here are some affirmations to embrace this mindset (Van Dijk, 2021):

- It's fine to feel as I do now.
- I have the right to feel this way.
- Feeling this doesn't dictate my actions.
- This will pass; for now, I feel this.
- This emotion is uncomfortable, yet harmless.

Choose three of your favorite affirmations and note them. When judging feelings, recite these aloud as a reminder of allowing the process.

Step 3

Understanding

In this final step, establish the context for your emotion. Pause to reflect on the events that led to this feeling. Avoid self-critique; focus on objective facts shaping your current state. Rather than self-judgment like "I was foolish, so I'm angry," opt for nonjudgmental analysis: "Given my fear of abandonment, it's natural to feel angry when calls aren't returned" (Van Dijk, 2021).

Level 2

Working on stronger emotions

Once you've practiced with mild emotions, extend the skill to an intense past event. Apply the initial three steps:

- Recall the emotion you felt.
- Envision how you'd allow this feeling, crafting a statement.
- Analyze the broader context and objective triggers for your emotions.

Level 1	
Acknowledging what I feel	
Statements that will help allow me to feel the emotion	
The reasons why I am feeling this way right now	
Level 2	
Naming the emotion I felt in this situation	
Statements I would've used to allow myself to feel the emotion	
The reasons I was feeling that way	

Emotion Exposure

Avoiding discomforting emotions often leads to harmful actions. This could stem from fear, an abusive upbringing, or a belief in emotion's futility. DBT aims to embrace emotions without fear. Negative emotions are natural. These steps aid in addressing avoided feelings, leading to diminished negative behaviors through practice (Dialectical Behavior Therapy, 2022).

Instructions

Step One: Identify Chronic Emotion

- Recall recurring problematic behaviors tied to a challenging emotion. Next, identify the underlying emotion causing these behaviors.
- Note emotion and the usual resulting behavior.

Step Two: Emotion Observation

- Stay alert throughout the day for the emergence of chronic emotions.
- Familiarize yourself with the exercise steps. Be prepared to implement the steps when emotion arises.

Step Three: Engage with Emotion

- When the emotion surfaces, allocate 5 minutes to sit and observe. Take deep breaths and note the emotion's intensity and bodily sensations.
- Embrace the discomfort; anticipate potential changes. Recognize shifts in an emotion's intensity or the emergence of other emotions (Dialectical Behavior Therapy, 2022).

Step Four: Embrace Inaction

- After observing the emotion's dynamics, experience just being with it.
- Explore how it feels to resist typical reactions. Remember, emotions are transient; informed handling surpasses automatic reactions (Dialectical Behavior Therapy, 2022).

Chronic emotion	
Observe the emotion	
Emotion exposure	
Emotion without action	

Final Words ...

Now, as you already know, DBT places a great emphasis on emotional validation. Central to this process is the cultivation of self-awareness. Through ongoing practice, individuals become attuned to the nuances of their emotions, discerning the triggers and patterns that propel them into distress. At the same time, it also deals with accepting your emotions. It means letting yourself feel your emotions without thinking they're good or bad. This doesn't mean you have to let emotions control you; rather, you're okay with having them. You learn from them and let them fade away on their own.

As we finish this chapter, remember that the goal of learning to deal with emotions and using DBT isn't to get rid of emotions. Emotions are a natural part of being human. Instead, it's about using their energy to help you grow and be well.

This journey means being aware of how you react and picking actions that help your long-term goals rather than just doing what you feel in the moment. This means changing bad behaviors into good ones and building stronger relationships by talking to and understanding others.

To sum it up, DBT gives you tools to build a real and meaningful life. It helps you control your emotions in a good way. This journey takes practice, patience, and a promise to get better. By following DBT, you're not just learning to handle emotions—you're also discovering more about yourself and finding a balance that makes your life better. But how can you find balance when you feel physically and emotionally distressed? Have you ever had an immediate emotional crisis that left you completely and totally stunned? For example, during recess, your friends would commonly hide each other's bags, and this time it was yours. But when it happened, you felt this urge to scream and cry. You felt rage throughout your body and mind and could not control it. This unfortunate incident directs us to the third core skill taught to teens in DBT. Can you guess what it is? To find out more, keep on reading!

Hello, I hope you have enjoyed this workbook. I would love to hear your thoughts on this book.

Many readers are unaware of how difficult it is to get reviews and how much they help authors like me.

I would greatly appreciate it if you could support me and help get the word out to other people about this book.

It is easy to leave a review, and I greatly appreciate every single review.

To leave a review please either scan the QR code or copy the link and paste it into a browser.

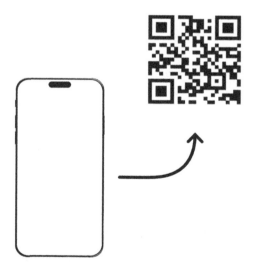

https://amzn.to/46i0YwV

CHAPTER 5:

BEYOND BREAKING POINT:
COPE. RESPOND POSITIVELY. REPEAT.

"The road to resilience is paved with the stones of distress, and it's our ability to walk that path that defines our journey."

- Unknown

In the unpredictable journey of life, storms are inevitable. Emotions can swell like turbulent waters, threatening to engulf our sense of balance and serenity. It's during these tempestuous times that distress tolerance becomes our guiding light, helping us not just survive but also thrive amidst emotional turmoil. Imagine distress tolerance as your life vest in the sea of emotions. It's the toolkit that equips you to stay afloat when faced with distressing situations. In this chapter, we'll dive deep into the essence of distress tolerance, exploring its significance and unveiling the strategies that can empower you to navigate emotional challenges with resilience and grace.

Distress tolerance is rooted in a foundation of acceptance and mindfulness, two of the major elements of DBT. It's not about suppressing or avoiding emotions but acknowledging them without judgment. We humans are quick to judge our emotions and put them into a negative context, but we forget that it is okay to feel overwhelmed or tired all the time. By embracing the discomfort and staying present, you're setting the stage for transformative growth that will help you understand your emotions, label them correctly, and weed out the problem that is causing such distress (Tull, 2020).

Let's take a look at Sarah's story to understand how distress tolerance can have a positive impact on a teenager's overall mental health.

Sarah was a spirited teenager with a heart full of dreams and a mind brimming with ambition. But life, like for many others, had its share of challenges. Exams, friendships, and family dynamics often threw her into emotional turmoil.

One day, as a particularly turbulent storm brewed both outside and within, Sarah decided it was time to put her distress tolerance strategies into practice. As the rain beat against her window, Sarah sat down with her journal, her safe haven for self-expression. She realized that distress was like a storm—it might shake you, but it wouldn't last forever.

With a deep breath, she began to write about her emotions, allowing herself to feel without judgment. Journaling is a great way of expressing her overflowing emotions. She recalled a distress tolerance technique she had learned: "Ride the Wave." Just like riding the ups and downs of the ocean, she decided to ride out her emotions without resisting or avoiding them. Avoiding emotions, especially negative ones, can have daunting effects on your mental health (Glosson, 2022).

Have you ever felt like nothing is going right in your life—your friends are ignoring you, you are failing classes, and your love life is falling apart?

But that's far from the truth. Our emotions can sometimes mislead us into a negative warzone in our heads. Sarah was smart enough to realize that whatever she felt in the moment would eventually pass.

Later that week, a conflict with her best friend left Sarah feeling hurt and angry. She felt the urge to lash out, but she remembered her distress tolerance skills. She decided to accept the situation.

She channeled her emotions into volunteering at a local animal shelter, immersing herself in giving back to others. One evening, after a heated argument with her parents, Sarah's stress levels soared. Instead of retreating to her room, she remembered the "TIP Skills": temperature, intense exercise, paced breathing. She decided to take a brisk walk around the block, breathing deeply and feeling the cool air on her skin. This simple act helped her regain a sense of calm and perspective.

The day of a major exam arrived, accompanied by a storm of nervousness. As Sarah sat down to write, she felt her heart race. But she knew that her distress tolerance toolbox held another technique: "self-soothe" (Glosson, 2022).

After the exam, she treated herself to her favorite warm cup of tea, wrapped herself in a cozy blanket, and let soothing music wash over her. This act of self-kindness eased her nerves and allowed her to re-center. With time, Sarah became the master of navigating life's emotional storms. She found that by embracing distress tolerance strategies, she could not only weather the hardships but also emerge from them with newfound strength. Each challenge was an opportunity to practice her skills, and as she did, she discovered a resilience within herself that she never knew existed. Through the rain and the sunshine, Sarah's journey helped her understand that even when the emotional tides are intense and high, they can be dealt with easily.

Moreover, mental health disorders such as borderline personality disorder (BPD) are tougher due to intense emotions. These feelings, such as sadness or anger, can cause both physical and emotional distress, quickly turning into a crisis. The distress causes a wide range of emotional chaos that is often difficult for teens, and sometimes even adults, to handle. Therefore, DBT places a great emphasis on dealing with stressful emotions through mindfulness. This approach offers an array of distress tolerance skills that serve as a lifeline, enabling you to grapple with intense emotions and prevent a downward spiral into crisis. By now, you must have understood the basics of distress tolerance. Sarah's experience gives you an overview of how, when you become tolerant of distress, you are able to manage so many things in your life. Still, why do DBT therapists place an emphasis on this particular element during dialectical therapy?

Why Is Distress Tolerance Important?

As you know, distress tolerance is a crucial psychological skill that enables individuals to effectively manage and cope with difficult or distressing situations. We have Sarah's experience to refer to. Similarly, it plays a significant role in keeping your mental health protected as well as your overall well-being. Here are several reasons why distress tolerance is important:

Enhanced Resilience

Have you ever felt powerless in the face of a challenge? Your hands become numb, and you are unable to move your body. That is stress settling in. So, DBT ensures that you use distress tolerance as an effective tool to build resilience in the face of adversity. It allows you to bounce back from setbacks, trauma, and stressors, making you better equipped to handle life's challenges. Life is a collection of hardships and brief moments of relief, so don't give up (Tull, 2020). You are braver than you can imagine. It's about time you accept the power that sits within you. Besides, resilience is a key factor in maintaining good mental health.

Improved Emotional Regulation

Emotional regulation is a key factor in maintaining a healthy life. As we have discussed in earlier chapters, when you regulate your emotions properly, you are able to navigate through difficult moments easily. Therefore, developing distress tolerance skills can help you manage your emotions more effectively. Instead of reacting impulsively to distressing situations, you can respond in a calmer and more rational manner. This ability to regulate emotions can prevent impulsive reactions to uncertainty, such as uncontrollable crying, aggression, etc. (Tull, 2020).

Reduction in Self-Destructive Behaviors

Many individuals turn to self-destructive behaviors like substance abuse, self-harm, or reckless actions when they cannot tolerate distress. Now, I understand that when you feel lost, the confusion of not being able to find your way out of the difficulty only makes things worse. Learning how to tolerate distress can significantly reduce the likelihood of engaging in such harmful behaviors, thereby promoting a healthier lifestyle. Once you are able to manage stress and find rational ways of dealing with any distressing situations, you will automatically feel lighter and calmer.

Effective Problem-Solving

Ironically, problems are always going to be a part of our lives, so learning how to deal with them quickly will help you solve them easily. This is where distress tolerance plays an important role. It encourages you to think clearly and logically, even when you are facing highly emotional or distressing situations. This can lead to better problem-solving skills, allowing you to find constructive solutions to your problems (Biswas, 2016).

Improved Interpersonal Relationships

Did you know that once you become tolerant of stressful situations, you get better at managing conflict altogether? Difficult situations are a part of the hamper package life delivers at your door every day, so one thing is clear: you cannot run away from them. Therefore, it's important to learn different ways that you can use to manage conflicts and maintain healthy relationships. With the help of distress tolerance, you can navigate challenging conversations without resorting to anger or avoidance, leading to more positive and meaningful connections with others.

Stress Reduction

When people can tolerate distress without becoming overwhelmed, they experience less chronic stress. I mean, it's obvious. Have you ever stayed up late at night, overthinking about a test that you are well-prepared for? It's like the anxiety of important facts slipping your mind intentionally keeps you up.

It's important for you to understand that having high levels of stress can cause various physical and mental health issues, including cardiovascular problems and anxiety disorders. Therefore, distress tolerance can help mitigate these negative effects.

Enhanced Coping Skills

Having sustainable coping mechanisms can help you recover from stressful events. In that case, distress tolerance is one of the best systems. It is essential not only for managing unwarranted crises but also for day-to-day stressors and challenges. A well-developed distress tolerance toolkit will allow you to cope more effectively with both acute and chronic stressors (Biswas, 2016).

Empowerment

An empowered teen can fight against all odds. So, it's important for you to incorporate skills such as distress tolerance so that you have a greater sense of control over your emotional responses and life circumstances. This empowerment can boost self-esteem and self-confidence, leading to a more positive self-concept.

Prevention of Mental Health Issues

During a talent show performance, have you ever felt a sense of stress wash all over you? Do you feel like your heart is beating faster than usual and your stomach is in knots? That's anxiety creeping onto you. High levels of distress intolerance are often linked to the development of various mental health conditions, such as depression and anxiety disorders. By improving distress tolerance, you can reduce their susceptibility to these conditions and enhance their overall mental health (Biswas, 2016).

Enhanced Quality of Life

Ultimately, distress tolerance contributes to an improved overall quality of life. When you are able to navigate life's challenges more effectively and maintain better mental and emotional well-being, you will be more likely to experience a fulfilling and satisfying life.

So, distress tolerance is an important skill that has far-reaching implications for mental health, emotional well-being, and overall quality of life. Developing and honing distress tolerance skills can empower individuals to navigate life's ups and downs with resilience, emotional regulation, and a greater sense of control, ultimately leading to a happier and healthier life.

I have an experience to share with you—it's David's story, and it will help you see why DBT therapists place such an emphasis on distress tolerance.

David was a high school junior who was known for his competitive spirit and dedication to his passion—swimming. David had his sights set on making the varsity swim team, and he trained tirelessly to achieve that goal. His daily routine included grueling swim practices, early morning workouts, and strict dieting to maintain his peak physical condition. Now, this routine is very tight and can easily turn into something stressful.

One day, as the tryouts for the varsity team approached, David felt the pressure mounting; it was as if his stomach was in knots so tight he could not undo them. His thoughts polluted his mind. He had invested so much time and effort into his training that the thought of not making the team was unbearable. The fear of failure consumed him, and his anxiety levels skyrocketed. In these moments, having a support system such as family and friends can make a huge difference.

His parents noticed the toll this stress was taking on David and sat down with him one evening to talk. His father, who had experience in competitive sports, shared a story from his own youth. "David," he said, "I remember the time I had to make the basketball team in high school. I was practicing day and night, just like you are now. But one day, I pushed myself too hard and ended up injuring my ankle" (Smith, 2019).

David listened intently as his father continued, "That injury taught me something crucial. It's essential to give your body and mind time to recover. Sometimes, when you're too focused on your goals, you can become your own worst enemy."

David's mother chimed in, "Sweetie, it's okay to be passionate about your dreams, but remember that distress tolerance isn't just about pushing through pain. It's also about knowing when to step back, take a breath, and regain your composure."

David absorbed his parents' words with patience and decided to approach his training differently. He started incorporating rest days into his routine, allowing his body to recover and rejuvenate. He also began practicing mindfulness and meditation techniques to manage his anxiety (Smith, 2019).

As the day of the varsity swim team tryouts arrived, David felt a sense of calm he hadn't experienced before. He knew he had done everything he could to prepare, but he also understood the importance of distress tolerance—knowing that even if things didn't go as planned, he could handle it.

David gave his all during the tryouts, and when the results were announced, he was thrilled to find his name on the varsity swim team roster. But what mattered most was that he had learned a valuable life lesson: the importance of balance, self-care, and the ability to withstand distress without crumbling under its weight.

DBT & Distress Tolerance

I have a confession—throughout each of these real-life examples, there are some easter eggs that point you toward important distress tolerance skills. Can you guess them? In Sarah's story, it is acceptance, and in David's story, it is radical acceptance.

DBT and distress tolerance have a unique pairing. Life is filled with pain and stress; therefore, they cannot be avoided. This is why DBT places an emphasis on learning skills that can help you deal with pain skillfully instead of giving up in the face of any challenge. As we have discussed earlier, distress tolerance is the ability to see through the fog of pain and perceive the situation as it is instead of demanding it to be different.

Acceptance of reality is an important part of DBT treatment; it helps you understand that when you are unable to sort out your emotions amidst a crisis, you'd have to rely on tolerating the stress before an impulsive reaction interferes. Here are six reasons why distress tolerance is a key skill to learn in your whole DBT journey:

Pst ... maybe I'll give you a bonus reason:

1. Emotion Regulation

By now, you must be aware of the urgency placed on emotional regulation by DBT. You know that DBT is primarily used for those who are struggling with intense emotions, often as a result of conditions like borderline personality disorder. However, it is also used for teens like yourself who are secretly battling stress and depression. In either case, distress tolerance is a key component in your DBT journey because it can help you manage your overwhelming emotions (DBT.tools, 2020). For example, once you build a mechanism using distress tolerance, you will be able to sit through a week of the testing process and come out with the best grades. In those moments where your mind would go blank, you'd have a fighting chance. By learning to tolerate distress, teens can prevent impulsive and harmful behaviors that may result from an inability to cope with intense feelings.

2. Reducing Stress and Negative Thoughts

One of the key goals of DBT is to reduce self-harming behaviors and suicidal tendencies, which are common among teens and young adults. Distress tolerance skills provide alternative coping mechanisms that allow teens to endure emotional pain without resorting to self-destructive actions. Now, I know that life can be difficult, but that does not mean that you will hurt yourself. Remember, you are not alone in this fight; you have people who love and support you, but be sure to reach out to them.

3. Crisis Management

Have you ever been in a situation where you felt like everything was spiraling out of control? In those moments, it's always helpful to take the back seat and understand where the situation is going. This is why DBT places an emphasis on distress tolerance, as it is essential for handling crisis situations effectively. In DBT, you are taught to use these skills when you encounter high-stress or emergency situations, for example, an SAT exam or an important interview with your dream university dean. This can help you avoid impulsive actions and make more rational decisions during moments of crisis.

4. Improved Interpersonal Relationship

Developing distress tolerance can lead to more stable and healthier interpersonal relationships. If you are someone who freaks out the moment something goes sideways in a friendship or a relationship, distress tolerance can help you stay away from impulsive reactions. Teens who can handle distressing emotions without reacting impulsively are better equipped to communicate effectively and resolve conflicts with others. For example, your girlfriend becomes upset because you forgot to wish her at 12 a.m. on her birthday, while you cannot move out of bed because you were so tired from football practice earlier. In that moment, instead of ghosting her or becoming defensive, you can rely on distress tolerance to help you communicate your situation better.

5. Love Life Better

By acquiring distress tolerance skills, you can experience an overall improvement in your quality of life. Life is all about enjoying the little moments of bliss it offers. When you are not seemingly worried about the worst possible things that can take you by surprise, like a pop quiz, unscheduled game practice, family fights, or a friend group breakup, you will see life for what it truly is—beautiful. You will become better equipped to face life's challenges, navigate difficult situations, and engage in fulfilling activities without being overwhelmed by distress.

6. Acceptance and Mindfulness

Distress tolerance skills often overlap with mindfulness techniques, which are another core component of DBT, as we have explored in the previous chapters. Mindfulness involves non-judgmental awareness of the present moment, and it helps teens accept their emotions without feeling the need to immediately change or react to them. This acceptance is crucial for distress tolerance because it allows individuals to experience their emotions without becoming consumed by them. (DBT.tools, 2020)

7. Long-Term Success

Here's a bonus tip that I promised:

In DBT, the goal is not just to provide short-term relief but to equip individuals with the skills they need to manage stress effectively in the long run. Therefore, it is a valuable tool that can be used throughout a person's life to navigate challenging situations and maintain emotional stability.

Now, for the moment that has been sitting patiently in the corner of your mind—here are three distress tolerance activities you can use to practice the skill by yourself:

DBT Activities

RESISTT Technique

What to Know

When emotions become overwhelming, responding in a healthy manner can be challenging. It's possible to turn to unhealthy coping mechanisms like overeating, alcohol consumption, or self-harm. DBT offers the RESISTT technique, consisting of seven skills, designed to assist you in dealing with these detrimental urges linked to distress. In distressing situations or crises, emotions can become almost unbearable, often leading individuals to seek solace in destructive habits (Dialectical Behavior Therapy, 2020).

RESISTT is a valuable tool for effectively managing distress and resisting behaviors that are detrimental to your well-being.

Use the following skills and choose one (or more) that's suitable for you:

1. Reframe the Situation

In moments of distress, you might find yourself thinking, "Life is awful," "I'll be stuck feeling like this forever," or "Things will never improve." Reframing your perspective can make a significant difference. By seeking the silver lining, it becomes easier to recognize that the situation may not be as dire as it initially appears. This approach isn't meant to dismiss the challenges you're facing; instead, it offers a means to view your circumstances in a more hopeful and grounded light (Dialectical Behavior Therapy, 2020).

2. Engage in a Distracting Activity

Pick an activity to thoughtfully engage in so you can distract yourself from the upsetting you.

3. Someone Else

If you focus your attention on another person, you can shift your attention to something other than your overwhelming emotions. Maybe you can help a loved one with a task, volunteer at a shelter, or listen when someone is telling their story.

4. Intense Sensations.

It can be helpful to distract yourself by experiencing safe, intense sensations. For example, take a cold shower or hot bath, or hold an ice cube in your hand. The idea is to experience intense sensations that aren't harmful.

5. Shut It Out

During a crisis, it's beneficial to step away from your immediate surroundings and relocate to a place where you can regain your composure, if feasible. After distancing yourself from the situation, if you find that your thoughts persistently dwell on it, consider whether you can actively address the problem at that moment. If the answer is affirmative, take action accordingly. However, if the answer is negative, imagine placing the issue in a container, setting it aside, and mentally "closing the door" to temporarily put it out of your mind (Dialectical Behavior Therapy, 2020).

6. Neutral Thoughts

Do something that won't add to your distress, like counting to ten, counting your breaths, or focusing on the colors of the objects around you. Sing your favorite song or repeat a phrase that seems helpful to you at the moment, like, "I can get through this because I am strong."

7. Take a Break

Maybe you can put off chores until tomorrow or take a day off work. Give yourself some time to calm down.

Here is a table that you can use to practice your skill:

Situation	
Reframing the situation	
Engaging in a distracting activity	
Someone else	
Intense sensation	
Shut it out	
Think neutral thoughts	
Take a break	

Radical Acceptance

Radical acceptance places a focus on accepting what you cannot change.

Step One: Acceptance

Let's embark on a journey within ourselves. Start by summoning an important event from your life—a memory that you find difficult to embrace. This could be something currently unfolding in your world or a past regret that still echoes within your thoughts. Take your time in selecting this memory, but if you've endured a traumatic event in the past, it's okay to set it aside for now. Choose an event that, while significant, won't overwhelm you as we delve into this process (Harris, 2022).

Step Two: What Caused It?

Now, let's explore the roots of this significant event. Delve deep into the details that led to its occurrence. As you do, remember not to pass judgment on yourself or lay blame on circumstances. For instance, if your chosen event revolves around the pain of being bullied in school, refrain from explaining it by saying the bullies were more popular or that you were labeled a "loser." These are judgments, not facts. Stick to the facts, free from value judgments (Harris, 2022). We're not trivializing your pain but seeking to gain a clearer perspective that can help you move forward.

Step Three: Embrace Your Emotions

As you reflect on this event, take notice of the emotions it stirs within you. Perhaps you're met with waves of frustration, anger, sadness, or shame. Be open to these emotions, and even try to detect physical sensations within your body that accompany them. It could be as noticeable as sweaty palms or a racing heart, or it might manifest in subtler ways. Regardless, fully accept these emotions as they are. Remember, you can't alter the past. Through wholehearted acceptance of your emotions and their bodily expressions, you'll begin to find a sense of relief (Harris, 2022).

Step Four: A Roadmap for Progress

In our final stride, we focus on crafting a proactive plan to address the situation or its lingering effects. If the event's impact is relatively insignificant in your life, practicing radical acceptance (as explored in the previous steps) may be sufficient to gradually come to terms with it. However, if this event has left a more substantial mark on you, ponder how you can enhance your circumstances. When uncertain about your next move, employ the mindfulness exercise of "Wise Mind" to guide you in shaping your path forward (Harris, 2022).

Here is an activity you can use with a "wise mind" to improve your emotional regulation:

Accepting Event
Important Event
What Caused the Event?
Accepting Emotions
Proactive Plan

TIPP

If you're ever swept away by a powerful emotional surge and feel unsure of how to manage it, this approach can provide assistance. Often, when teens find themselves engulfed in such situations, their capacity for rational thinking diminishes, and they become absorbed in their emotional state rather than their wise minds. TIPP is an acronym that encompasses the following four steps:

T: Temperature

Much like one of the earlier methods we've discussed, the initial step involves altering your body's temperature.

Lower temperatures have a calming effect on your heart rate, which tends to race during moments of emotional overwhelm. You can achieve this by splashing your face with cold water, taking a moderately cold shower, or, if the weather permits, going for a brisk walk outside. Another option is to hold an ice cube or gently rub it on your skin (Rosenthal, 2023).

Conversely, warmer temperatures can raise your heart rate, which is typically lower during periods of sadness, depression, or anxiety. To counter this, you can indulge in a warm bath, wrap yourself in a cozy blanket, bask in the sun on a hot day, or sip on a warm cup of tea.

Please exercise caution and use common sense. There's no need to go to extremes like a polar plunge. Cold exposure can cause a drop in blood pressure, while heat exposure can elevate it. If you have a medical condition that could be affected, you may want to skip this step or consult your healthcare provider.

I: Intense Exercise

When you're harboring pent-up energy due to overwhelming emotions, it can be highly beneficial to channel that energy through cardiovascular exercise. You don't need fancy equipment or a pricey gym membership; all you need is the willingness to get moving. Try one of the following: a brisk run around your neighborhood, some vigorous jumping jacks in your room, a fast-paced outdoor walk, skipping rope, dancing, or even weightlifting if you have the necessary equipment. Aim for 10–15 minutes, but don't overexert yourself. As you expend this stored energy, you'll likely feel more tired and find your overwhelming emotions becoming more manageable (Rosenthal, 2023).

P: Paced Breathing

To mitigate the physical manifestations of overwhelming emotions, such as an accelerated heart rate, flushed face, dry mouth, or sweating, try regulating your breathing to gradually reduce these symptoms. Attempt the following technique: take slow, deep breaths through your nose (utilizing abdominal breathing) for four seconds, and then exhale slowly through your mouth for 6 seconds. Dedicate 1–2 minutes to this practice (Footprints Community, 2020).

P: Progressive Muscle Relaxation

For relaxation of tense muscles during episodes of extreme emotions, consider progressive muscle relaxation. You can do this from a seated position. Start at the top of your body, consciously engaging the muscles in your upper back, tensing them for five seconds, and then releasing. Progress to your arms, your abdominal and back muscles, your buttocks, thighs, upper legs, and finally, your calves. This exercise helps your body release the excess energy accumulated during moments of emotional overwhelm (Footprints Community, 2020).

Here is a table that you can customize while practicing distress tolerance with TIPP:

Situation	
Step 1 – Temperature	
Step 2 – Intense emotions	
Step 3 – Paced breathing	
Step 4 – Progressive muscle relaxation	
How did this technique help me?	
Level of emotional distress before exercise (1–10)	
Level of emotional distress after exercise (1–10)	

Final Words ...

All in all, distress tolerance is an integral and transformative component of DBT. It equips individuals with the essential skills to navigate the turbulent waters of intense emotions, crises, and challenging situations.

As you saw throughout this chapter, by mastering distress tolerance, individuals can prevent impulsive and harmful reactions, effectively manage their emotions, reduce self-destructive behaviors, and ultimately lead more balanced and fulfilling lives. DBT recognizes that distress is an inevitable part of the human experience, and through the cultivation of these skills, individuals can learn not only to endure distress but to emerge from it with resilience, wisdom, and a renewed sense of self.

Now, we are slowly approaching the end of the book with our last core skill. Are you excited? I'm sure you are! Have you ever felt like your actions have an inconsequential effect on your relationships, and it usually turns the whole tone negative?

If yes, you might need to work on your interpersonal skills. Let me teach you how you can positively change your behaviors to have better relationships.

CHAPTER 6:

BREAKING BARRIERS:
THE MAGIC OF COMMUNICATION

"The way you communicate with others and the way you handle difficult conversations determines the kind of relationships you have."

- Deepak Chopra

In life, communication is key; it's that simple, especially when it comes to relationships. Have you ever felt a slight change in your friend's tone, sending your anxiety through the roof? Or do you feel like lately, whatever you say to your family is misinterpreted? Don't worry; you are about to understand why this is the case and how you can create a positive space for yourself by changing a few habits.

Effective communication is an essential life skill that is often overlooked by people because they are busy hustling in life. Don't get me wrong. I'm not against making the most out of life, but our relationships are delicate and demanding. Some days, your friends would say or do something that would hurt your feelings. If you do not communicate effectively what hurts you and why, you will be left with nothing but resentment in your life for them. Eventually, the bitter aftertaste would turn into distance, and you will lose a friend.

So, as humans, we're naturally drawn to one another—the one way you connect with others is through the delightful dance of communication across various situations. Think of it like this: every day, you don different hats, playing various roles depending on the context of your interactions. But here's the secret that makes these exchanges truly click—clear and effective communication (The Scientific World, 2020).

So, at the very heart of a successful relationship lies effective communication. I know that you want to build meaningful and lasting connections; however, the essential ingredient of this is communication. So, there are a few elements that I want you to remember before we dive into how DBT comes into play.

First up, you have to recognize intriguing body language cues. It's like deciphering a secret code that reveals a world of unspoken thoughts and feelings. For example, you are in between conversations with a new friend, and they keep on looking elsewhere. This means that they are not that interested in that conversation; however, if they are listening attentively and nodding at some of the opinions that you share, they are interested and hooked. Moreover, you'll have to focus on the art of effective listening—not just hearing words but really tuning in to what's being said and unsaid (Corporate Finance Institute, 2018).

When you get the hang of these elements, something magical happens. Your social interactions start to sparkle, your confidence in engaging with others skyrockets, and you'll even find yourself acing class presentations and forging those long-lasting relationships that light up your life. So, let's explore these gems of wisdom and watch your communication skills become the key to unlocking a world of possibilities. I want to share Annie's experience with you so that you are able to understand the emphasis placed on interpersonal skills by DBT specialists.

Annie's Story

Personal growth and resilience are two elements that are often missing from a teen's life, majorly because they are bombarded by pressure. Annie was no different, even though she was just seventeen years old, but her life had already been a rollercoaster of emotions, challenges, and self-discovery. Annie's journey began with two formidable adversaries: depression and substance abuse disorder. Now, I understand that for most of you, these terms can be sensitive and even triggering, but bear with me. I am trying to help you understand that recovery is a part of healing and that there is nothing wrong with accepting your past. In order for you to move on from your past mistakes, you will have to accept them. Annie was stuck in a cycle of emotional abuse; she would often become overly self-critical, which forced her into drugs (Newroads, 2018).

However, Annie's family was her unwavering support system, standing by her side through thick and thin, but they, too, felt the weight of helplessness as Annie's addiction continued to grip her. Her depression had grown so profound that it seemed to swallow her whole, causing her to withdraw from the world, especially her family.

Annie's life was marked by conflicts with her parents, whose desperation to help her had driven them to react with anxiety and frustration. As her despair deepened, Annie's days became a haze of despair and anger, with yelling becoming her desperate cry for help. Remember the question I asked you in the beginning? "Have you ever felt like you were being misunderstood by your parents?" It's common for people to get lost in conversations, especially under stressful situations such as Annie's. It's ten times harder to find the right words that can convince your family that you are trying.

Determined to find a solution, Annie's parents embarked on a quest to discover an inpatient program specializing in dual diagnosis and evidence-based treatments. Annie was soon admitted to an inpatient facility designed for young women aged 17 to 28, where she would embark on a life-changing journey guided by DBT.

How did DBT help Annie?

DBT was the key that unlocked the door to Annie's transformation. It began with identifying the problematic behavioral patterns at the heart of her struggles—patterns that had disrupted her ability to function in all aspects of life. Throughout this learning experience, you are also preparing for your transformation. I'm excited for you.

Anyway, with a structured hierarchy targeting behaviors that threatened Annie's well-being and quality of life, DBT provided the framework for her recovery (Newroads, 2018).

How did she use DBT?

From suicidal thoughts and self-harming to excessive substance use, this stage aimed to tame the wild torrent of her emotions and steer her toward behavioral control. Annie had to learn that control was not a distant dream but a reachable reality.

One of the treasures Annie uncovered in DBT was the art of "interpersonal effectiveness." This skill guided her in forming positive and productive connections with others. Annie learned the art of effective communication, understanding that her relationships were like sails catching the winds of her emotions. By mastering this skill, she transformed her rocky connections into smoother, more harmonious interactions.

During this time, Annie was brought face-to-face with a life she thought was beyond reach. Despite regaining control of her behavior, a feeling of failure still loomed. Therefore, along with communication, she worked on emotional regulation, where she was able to understand, manage, and, most importantly, communicate emotions effectively once more.

The next step in her rediscovery was to address her emotions. Annie yearned to feel alive again, her emotions having been numbed by substances. The therapist, recognizing her talent for poetry, nurtured it, helping Annie see her own strength through her writing. The power of mindfulness and meditation became apparent, allowing Annie to balance her rational and emotional mind while also deepening her interpersonal connection through the essential skill of communication. Moreover, when you are mindful and calm, you think before you react or even speak, which makes the whole communication process smoother.

The last stage of her journey was a gateway to spiritual fulfillment. Annie, like many others, found solace in believing in guardian angels who protected her during the darkest moments of her life. She had survived accidents and overdoses, and she saw these as signs that something greater watched over her. At the end of the day, Annie's mental and physical health became a priority for her and her family, which resulted in a fruitful journey of recovery with DBT.

As Annie's journey in the inpatient program came to an end, she emerged as a phoenix from the ashes. With the support of her family and her newfound skills, she returned to her life with renewed vigor. She left behind the crutch of pain medication, resumed her education, and chose to pursue a degree in English. Her creative writing class, in particular, kept her mindful of her gift for crafting poetry. Her words became her most prized possession; she not only learned how to use them in writing but also how she could use them to communicate effectively and maintain healthy relationships with her loved ones (Newroads, 2018).

And so, Annie's story became a testament to the power of resilience, family support, and the transformative potential of DBT. With her guardian angels watching over her, she embarked on a brighter, more hopeful chapter in the book of her life, proving that even in the darkest of times, there is light at the end of the tunnel. Annie's story is an inspiration to me, particularly! This is mainly true because she was able to fight all the odds stacked against her and emerge successful. She realized that she needed help and did her due diligence in completing the program; her consistency and dedication helped her recover effectively.

Now, I am sure you must be curious to know more about interpersonal effectiveness. Have you asked yourself—what is the most important skill that I can have? I bet if I asked you to make a list, you'd come up with a few, right?

There is a whole list of skills that you can add to your repertoire. You will always find thousands of resources at the tips of your fingers, waiting to be explored so that you can learn a new skill or improve the one you already possess.

But which one is most important?

There might not be a definitive answer to this question, but I think the most common answer that I have come across is "communication," aka interpersonal skills. To be able to communicate with people effectively is an art that so many teens and adults are looking to learn.

So, how can you define interpersonal effectiveness?

Interpersonal effectiveness is like the magic key to unlocking successful human interactions. It's all about mastering the art of clear and thoughtful communication, whether you're expressing your own thoughts and needs assertively, actively listening to others, or empathizing with their feelings. It's the skill of gracefully resolving conflicts, setting and respecting personal boundaries, and keeping emotions in check. It's about adapting your approach to different social situations and, above all, treating everyone with respect and tolerance, even in the face of differences. In essence, interpersonal effectiveness is your secret weapon for building meaningful connections and thriving in the intricate dance of human relationships.

Interpersonal Skills

So, it's safe to say that it is a fundamental aspect of human interaction that encompasses a wide range of skills essential for successful social interactions, such as presentations, speech competitions, etc. (Ackerman & Wilson, 2017). These skills include:

Attending Relationships

Have you ever felt ignored or unheard in an interaction because the person you are with is distracted? One of the best things that can come out of incorporating interpersonal effectiveness is being present and emotionally available during interactions. It includes actively listening, showing empathy, and being responsive to the needs and emotions of others.

Balancing Priorities vs. Demands

Interpersonal effectiveness requires the ability to strike a balance between the various demands and priorities that arise in different social situations. For example, if you are stuck between studying for your SAT, which is due next week, and going on your family vacation, which is more important? Your SAT score will help you get into your dream university, which should be your priority. I know that you want to go on trips with your family; this is where interpersonal skills play an integral role. You will have to communicate to your family that you'd like to delay the trip for another week so that you can enjoy it to the fullest. Therefore, interpersonal skills help you make thoughtful decisions about how to allocate your time and resources to meet both personal and external demands.

Balancing the "Wants" and the "Shoulds"

It involves reconciling your personal desires and needs with your obligations and responsibilities. This skill allows you to make choices that align with your values and long-term goals while addressing immediate wants (Ackerman & Wilson, 2017).

Building a Sense of Mastery and Self-Respect

Developing a healthy sense of self-esteem and self-worth is crucial for effective interpersonal interactions. It involves recognizing your own strengths and limitations and fostering a positive self-image. You are able to create healthy boundaries with the people around you so that you are not taken for granted.

Now, let's explore three different settings where you can use interpersonal effectiveness. So, our ability to interact with others is influenced by the specific goals we set for our interactions. In this regard, there are three primary objectives in interpersonal interactions:

Gaining Your Objective

When your primary focus is to achieve a specific outcome, you need to employ interpersonal skills that will enable you to clearly define your objectives for the interaction. This includes setting clear goals and devising strategies to attain them. For example, when in a study group, you need to clearly communicate your reasons for joining the group and stay clear of any distractions.

Maintaining Your Relationships

In certain situations, preserving and nurturing your relationships takes precedence. To achieve this goal, you must consider the significance of the relationship, strive to maintain healthy boundaries with the other person, and take actions that contribute to the longevity and quality of the relationship (Jouany, 2023).

Keeping Your Self-Respect

Sometimes, our primary aim is to safeguard our own self-esteem and integrity. This objective necessitates using interpersonal skills to ensure that we leave an interaction feeling good about ourselves and in alignment with our values and truth.

It's important to note that different interpersonal skills may be more relevant depending on the specific goal we are striving to achieve in a given interaction. For instance:

- When pursuing your objectives, effective communication, negotiation, and problem-solving skills are crucial.
- For maintaining relationships, skills related to active listening, empathy, and compromise come to the forefront.
- In the pursuit of self-respect, assertiveness, boundary-setting, and ethical conduct become paramount. These are essential elements that need attention when you are rebuilding yourself (Jouany, 2023).

With that being said, interpersonal effectiveness is a multifaceted concept that encompasses skills vital for navigating the complex web of human interactions. Whether our focus is on achieving objectives, nurturing relationships, or preserving our self-respect, honing these skills empowers us to engage with others in a manner that aligns with our intentions and values.

Why Is Interpersonal Effectiveness Important?

By now, you are well aware of how you can define an interpersonal skill. However, it's equally important to understand why it's a crucial life skill. They are extremely important for creating and maintaining meaningful personal relationships with your family and friends. People with good interpersonal communication skills can, therefore, build healthy relationships with their family members, peers, relatives, and friends. Here are a few reasons why interpersonal effectiveness is a game-changer for people undergoing DBT and regulating their emotions:

Healthy Relationships

Effective interpersonal skills are the foundation of healthy and fulfilling relationships. They allow you to communicate openly, resolve conflicts constructively, and build trust and intimacy with others. For example, you are able to communicate your emotions to your friends effectively when they do not invite you to a spontaneous plan or when one of them has hurt your feelings.

Effective Communication

Good communication is at the heart of all successful relationships. Interpersonal effectiveness equips you with the tools to express your thoughts, feelings, and needs clearly and to understand others' perspectives. Let's say you were upset about a disagreement you had with your sibling. In order for both of you to move on, it's important to have a constructive feedback session where both of you are able to process the situation and put your opinions forward. The end goal is to achieve reconciliation.

Conflict Resolution

Life is full of conflicts, both big and small. Some days, your brothers will annoy you, while on others, you will be frustrated by something your best friend did. Interpersonal effectiveness empowers you to navigate these conflicts in a way that promotes understanding and cooperation rather than escalating tension. You will have more control over the conversations after a steaming argument (Jouany, 2023).

Personal Well-Being

Have you ever felt like, after an intense argument with a classmate, you could not bring yourself to go to school the next day? Your ability to interact effectively with others directly impacts your mental and emotional well-being. Healthy relationships and effective communication can reduce stress, anxiety, and feelings of isolation (Ackerman & Wilson, 2017).

Career Success

We all want to be successful when we grow up. I'm sure you have aspirations to be wealthy and successful, but success isn't easy. Let me give you a head start!

In the professional world, interpersonal effectiveness is a key skill. It helps you build strong working relationships with colleagues, clients, and supervisors, which can lead to career advancement and job satisfaction.

Self-Esteem and Confidence

When you can assert yourself respectfully, maintain boundaries, and handle social situations with grace, it boosts your self-esteem and self-confidence. Interpersonal effectiveness contributes to a positive self-image (Ackerman & Wilson, 2017).

Life Satisfaction

Successful interactions with others enhance your overall quality of life. Meaningful connections, supportive friendships, and loving relationships are essential components of a satisfying life. This way, you are able to live life to its fullest.

Adaptability

Being able to adapt your communication style to different situations and personalities makes you more flexible and better equipped to handle various social contexts. For example, you had a bad day in school, and you came home to your mother, who was equally upset. Instead of being angry with her, if you use empathy in communicating with her, you will be able to change the whole course of your and her day ahead.

Conflict Prevention

Interpersonal effectiveness not only helps in resolving conflicts but also in preventing them. By effectively expressing yourself and understanding others, you can address issues before they escalate.

Personal Growth

Developing interpersonal skills is a journey of self-discovery and personal growth. It encourages you to reflect on your communication patterns, understand your emotions better, and continuously improve your interactions with others (Ackerman & Wilson, 2017).

There you have it—the importance of interpersonal skills.

Now you know that interpersonal effectiveness is the linchpin of successful, fulfilling, and harmonious human interactions. It enriches your personal and professional life, enhances your well-being, and supports your journey toward becoming the best version of yourself. Whether in relationships, the workplace, or daily life, mastering these skills can open doors to opportunities and enrich your overall experience. So, now that you understand the basics let's dive deeper into how DBT makes use of interpersonal effectiveness as a core skill in helping teens change their lives.

DBT & Interpersonal Effectiveness

Interpersonal effectiveness is about achieving goals in relationships. This includes meeting your needs, convincing others to support your desires, and making them take your opinions seriously. The ultimate goal is to strengthen existing relationships, build new ones, and leave toxic ones when needed. Balancing connection, change, and acceptance is vital.

But remember, mastering these skills takes effort. Emotions can make it tough to build healthy relationships, and negative thoughts about ourselves can hinder us. So, becoming skilled in interpersonal effectiveness is a learned journey, but it's a journey worth taking. Here are a few ways DBT makes use of interpersonal effectiveness:

Relationship Functioning

DBT recognizes that interpersonal relationships play a significant role in an individual's well-being. The quality of your relationships can have an impact on your emotional regulation, self-esteem, and overall life satisfaction. By enhancing interpersonal effectiveness, DBT aims to improve relationships and, consequently, the individual's mental health (DBT.tools, 2020).

Emotional Regulation

As you already know, emotional regulation is a major part of DBT. So, interpersonal skills are closely tied to emotional regulation. You might experience intense emotions in the context of relationships, and these emotions can be triggers for eruptive behaviors. Interpersonal effectiveness skills help individuals manage their emotions during interactions, reducing impulsive or self-destructive reactions (DBT.tools, 2020).

Conflict Resolution

Conflicts are a natural part of human relationships; you cannot escape the inevitable. However, in DBT, you learn how to navigate conflicts constructively rather than reactively. Interpersonal effectiveness equips you with the tools to communicate assertively, empathize with others, and find solutions that are mutually satisfying. This can prevent conflicts from escalating and causing further emotional distress. For example, if you want to change your subjects in school, this leads you into a conflict with your parents. In this situation, communicating why you are switching and what the long-term benefits will be is the key.

Interpersonal Triggers

Certain individuals or situations can serve as triggers for emotional dysregulation and behaviors. DBT can identify these triggers and develop strategies to manage them effectively. By improving interpersonal skills, you can reduce the emotional impact of triggering situations and maintain a greater sense of control (DBT.tools, 2020).

Validation and Support

DBT emphasizes the importance of validation in relationships. You cannot go far without validating the feelings and emotions of your friends and family members after a fight or conflict. We, as humans, do not dictate how someone feels; therefore, it's important to let emotions flow and respect them. Interpersonal effectiveness skills teach individuals how to validate their own emotions and the emotions of others. This validation fosters a sense of understanding and support within relationships, which can be particularly beneficial for individuals struggling with emotional dysregulation or self-esteem issues.

Behavioral Change

DBT is often used to address behaviors that are harmful or self-destructive, such as self-harm or substance abuse. Interpersonal effectiveness skills provide individuals with alternative ways of coping with distress and seeking support from others rather than resorting to harmful behaviors. Through interpersonal skills, you are able to communicate to your loved ones that you need support.

Effective Communication

Effective communication is a cornerstone of DBT's interpersonal effectiveness. Learning how to express thoughts, feelings, and needs clearly and assertively reduces misunderstandings and promotes better outcomes in relationships. This is especially important for individuals who may have a history of communication difficulties or conflicts.

Building a Support System

DBT encourages you to build a network of supportive relationships. Interpersonal effectiveness skills help you establish and maintain these connections, whether with family members, friends, or therapists. A strong support system is vital for individuals undergoing DBT, as it provides a safety net during challenging times.

Goal Attainment

As you know, DBT often involves setting and working toward specific goals, both in therapy and in daily life. Interpersonal effectiveness skills are essential for achieving these goals, as they enable individuals to negotiate, collaborate, and advocate for their needs effectively. This can be particularly important when seeking help or resources to support recovery and well-being (DBT. tools, 2020).

Integration with Other DBT Core Skills

Interpersonal effectiveness is not isolated within DBT but is integrated with other skills, such as emotion regulation and distress tolerance. This integration reinforces the idea that interpersonal skills are essential for managing emotions, handling crises, and making lasting behavioral changes.

Now, for the moment that has been sitting patiently at the corner of your mind—here are 3 interpersonal activities that you can use to practice the skill by yourself. These are endorsed by DBT specialists, so you are in luck!

DBT Activities

DEARMAN

DEARMAN is an acronym used in dialectical behavior therapy (DBT) as a tool to foster effective interpersonal communication and assertiveness. Each letter in DEARMAN stands for a step to follow in interactions where one needs to make a request or say no: "Describe," "Express," "Assert," "Reinforce," "Mindful," "Appear confident," and "Negotiate." The method aims to help individuals communicate their needs or decline requests in a respectful and effective manner, thus facilitating healthy relationships and conflict resolution. It aims to enhance your ability to communicate effectively in your interactions with others, ultimately assisting you in meeting your needs and fostering positive and healthy relationships. It will teach you about effective communication, especially in challenging or emotionally charged situations. By breaking down the communication process into specific steps, it helps individuals express themselves clearly and assertively. Moreover, it will help establish and maintain healthy boundaries in your relationships and finally provide a structured approach to communication that reduces the likelihood of conflicts and misunderstandings. By using this technique, individuals can address issues in a respectful and constructive manner. You can use DEAR MAN to practice emotional regulation and healthy boundary development.

Use the table below to practice and document your skill:

Describe	
Express	
Assert	
Reinforce	
Mindful	
Appear	
Negotiate	

GIVE

The GIVE skill is especially important for maintaining healthy relationships through effective communication. By using the GIVE technique, individuals can de-escalate conflicts and improve their ability to resolve disagreements. It helps prevent arguments from spiraling out of control. It also fosters healthier and more positive relationships by promoting empathy, understanding, and validation. It can lead to better rapport with friends, family members, and colleagues. Many individuals with emotional regulation difficulties struggle with intense emotional reactions in interpersonal situations. Here are what the acronyms mean and how you can incorporate them in your life:

(be) Gentle:
- Show respect and avoid attacks, threats, and manipulation.
- Express anger directly and calmly.
- Avoid judgment and disrespectful gestures.

(act) Interested:
- Actively listen and maintain eye contact.
- Avoid interrupting and show genuine interest.

Validate:

- Demonstrate understanding and empathy.
- Acknowledge the other person's feelings and perspective.

(use an) Easy Manner:

- Add humor and maintain a friendly tone.
- Smile and be diplomatic.

Take a difficult situation and use this table to practice this technique:

Gentle	
Interested	
Validate	
Easy Manner	

FAST

The FAST activity is an important component of communication as it allows you to maintain your self-respect and requires you to be truthful about the problems (even if you are tactful about how you frame them) and not sacrifice your values or integrity. So, here is how you can use the activity FAST in your life:

Be Fair

Be fair to yourself and to the other person.

Don't Over-Apologize

No apologizing for being alive or for making a request at all. Make no apologies for having an opinion or for disagreeing.

Stick to Your Values

Don't sell out your values or integrity for reasons that aren't very important. Be clear on what you believe is the moral or valued way of thinking.

Be Truthful

Don't lie. Don't act helpless when you are not. Don't exaggerate or make up excuses.

This will help you communicate your emotions effectively and maintain healthy relationships with the people you love.

Final Words ...

Interpersonal effectiveness stands as an indispensable pillar within the framework of DBT. Its significance lies in its capacity to empower individuals to navigate the intricate web of human relationships, fostering healthy connections, managing conflicts constructively, and enhancing emotional well-being.

In the journey toward self-discovery and personal growth, these skills enable individuals to communicate effectively, set boundaries, and make choices that align with their values. Through the lens of DBT, interpersonal effectiveness is not just a set of skills; it is the catalyst for profound transformation, facilitating the pursuit of a more balanced, fulfilling, and resilient life.

So, now that you are well aware of all the core skills of DBT, are you ready to do some basic exercises? Turn the page, and let's get to work!

CHAPTER 7:

PRACTICE MAKES PERFECT: TAKING IT ONE DAY AT A TIME

"And once you understand that habits can change, you have the freedom and the responsibility to remake them."

- Charles Duhigg

Imagine crafting habits that stick as firmly as your favorite song's catchy tune. Just as a song plays 21 days on repeat to etch itself into your memory, this rule promises to guide you through 21 days of habit formation, setting the stage for 90 days of effortless habit mastery. It's the rhythm of your life's playlist, where good habits become your greatest hits! So, 21/90 is one of the ways you can change your life (Love Wellness, 2020). Remember, when you set your mind to changing your habits, take smaller steps toward your end goal; lunging to your destination will teach you nothing. In fact, it will exhaust you in the end.

Healthy Habits

Here is a list of activities that you can do to turn your life upside down and engage in good habits:

Mindfulness: Go for a Walk

Let's dive into mindfulness—a simple yet transformative practice. If you remember, mindfulness is one of the major core skills of DBT, and for the right reasons. If you are not mindful of what you do and how you live life, you will eventually get lost. Here are a few ways you can reconnect with yourself:

- Step outside and take a walk. Feel the ground beneath your feet, the rhythm of your breath, and embrace the world around you. Notice the colors of the sky, the buildings, and the foliage.
- Breathe in the scents of the environment. Observe the leaves dancing in the wind. Give words to your observations, describing what you see and smell.
- If your mind wanders, that's okay. Don't label it as good or bad; just acknowledge it and gently redirect your focus.

Reality Acceptance

DBT introduces the concept of reality acceptance—a powerful tool for living life on life's terms. Again, acceptance and validation are two leading pillars of DBT; therefore, accepting reality ensures that you are able to make informed decisions. Here are a few ways you can incorporate this healthy habit in your life:

- It's about embracing both the pleasant and less-than-ideal moments that life offers us. Resisting reality only intensifies our suffering. For instance, when you're stuck in traffic and itching to get home, instead of letting frustration take over, remind yourself that there's little you can do about it right now.

- You're not in control of the traffic, and it's a common occurrence during rush hour. Others around you share the same goal—getting home. Accepting this reality can surprisingly ease your frustration.

Non-Judgmental Stance

A non-judgmental stance is a crucial skill for taming intense emotions like anger. Often, we label things as "good" or "bad," creating emotional turmoil and straining relationships. Self-judgment can be particularly painful.

- When you catch yourself making judgments, pause and simply notice, refraining from judging your judgments!
- Take the example of gloomy weather; instead of criticizing it as awful, tell yourself, "It's raining, and I'm feeling irritated because I might get cold and wet." This doesn't change the weather, but it prevents you from letting it dictate your entire day (Nasca, 2021).

Mindful Activities

Now, circling back to mindfulness, let's see how you can incorporate mindfulness into your life to its fullest extent. Here are three instances where you can incorporate mindfulness in your life:

1. Mindful Wakeup

Start your day with a purpose. Align your conscious thinking with your primal motivations, like connection, purpose, and core values. Sit in a relaxed posture, close your eyes, and breathe deeply for a few moments. Ask yourself, "What is my intention for today?" Reflect on how you can show up to have a positive impact and strengthen your mindset. Set your intention for the day, such as being kind, patient, or resilient. Throughout the day, pause and revisit your intention to enhance your interactions and mood.

2. Mindful Eating

Savor your meals mindfully. Before you begin eating, take a moment to breathe deeply and transition calmly to your meal. Listen to your body's hunger cues without overthinking or checking the time. Eat according to your hunger level and choose foods that truly satisfy you. Practice peaceful eating by slowing down and staying relaxed during your meals. If you don't enjoy a particular food, take your first few bites mindfully and decide if it's worth continuing.

3. Mindful Pause

Engage your "slow brain" with mindfulness. Recognize that much of our behavior operates on autopilot, but mindfulness can activate your executive control (Westside DBT, 2021). To shift the balance, create obstacles for your "fast brain" habits, like placing reminders in your way. Refresh these cues regularly to keep them effective. Develop new patterns with "If this, then that" messages to prompt intentional actions. As you practice deliberate and mindful actions, you strengthen your "slow brain" and promote neuroplasticity.

4. Mindful Workout

Transform your workout into a mindfulness practice. Whether you're biking, weightlifting, or swimming, exercise can become a mindful experience. Begin by setting a clear intention for your activity and visualizing how you want to engage with it. Warm up with rhythmic movements that synchronize with your breath. Find your rhythm and gradually challenge yourself to stay alert and energized. Cool down and reflect on your body's sensations. Take a moment to rest and acknowledge your feelings, fostering a mind-body connection (Westside DBT, 2021).

5. Mindful Driving

Stay calm during traffic with mindful driving. Heavy traffic often triggers stress and road rage. Shift your response by taking a deep breath to create space between the stimulus and your reaction. Identify what you need in that moment—whether it's safety, ease, or relief. Provide yourself with what you need, like releasing tension or offering self-compassion phrases. Recognize that all drivers share similar desires for safety, ease, and happiness. Offer them kind intentions, such as "May you be safe, may you feel at ease, may you be happy" (Westside DBT, 2021). Breathe deeply and transform your mood in seconds by focusing on your chosen intention.

Final Words ...

This chapter has served as a gateway into the realm of dialectical behavior therapy (DBT), offering teens a collection of uncomplicated yet highly effective activities that seamlessly integrate this therapeutic approach into their daily lives.

Each activity that is detailed above is easy to do and even easier to incorporate into your lives. At the end of the day, DBT stresses taking smaller steps to achieve a large difference in your lives.

Through these accessible exercises, you are provided with a bridge to understanding and embracing DBT, ultimately becoming more at ease with the concepts and techniques it entails. What makes these activities truly remarkable is their subtlety; they operate in the background, subtly and consistently nudging us toward self-improvement. For example, exercising does not have to be extensive or intensive; instead, go out for a jog or a walk. The idea is to get your body moving so that you can feel more energetic.

As you embark on this journey of self-discovery and personal growth, it will become increasingly clear that the transformation you seek does not need to be overt or grand. Instead, it can organically manifest, shaping a better version of ourselves without us even realizing it. So, through this chapter and the ones above, you can unlock the door to a more mindful, resilient, and enriched way of living—one that empowers you to navigate life's challenges with grace and resilience.

This marks the end of our journey together and the beginning of your transformative quest!

Hello, I hope you have enjoyed this workbook.
I would love to hear your thoughts on this book.

Many readers are unaware of how difficult it is to get reviews and how much they help authors like me.

I would greatly appreciate it if you could support me and help get the word out to other people about this book.

It is easy to leave a review, and I greatly appreciate every single review.

To leave a review please either scan the QR code or copy the link and paste it into a browser.

https://amzn.to/46i0YwV

CONCLUSION

So, here we are at the end of the road, and as we part ways, I want to tell you something—the skills that you have learned here are not the solution but mere tools. You are the solution to your problems.

Life is merciless; it will throw one problem after another at you, so with the help of these tools, you will have to restore your confidence in fighting life's uncharted battles.

Let's take a moment to reflect on the profound impact this journey can have on your life. We've embarked on a path that equips you with invaluable skills, not just to cope with life's challenges but to truly thrive in the face of adversity.

DBT isn't just another therapeutic approach; it's a comprehensive toolkit that empowers you to navigate the complex landscape of emotions, relationships, and personal growth. Throughout this book, you've been introduced to an array of strategies and techniques designed to foster self-awareness, emotional regulation, interpersonal effectiveness, and acceptance. I'm sure you would have understood the importance of DBT from Chapter 1. It dives deep into the peripherals of DBT and why you should choose it. You also understood the causes and reasons for your stress and potential triggers that were outlined in Chapter 2. At the end of the day, you need to be able to identify what bothers you and weed it out of your life.

Moving on, one of the core lessons you've learned is the art of mindfulness, which was explored in Chapter 4. Mindfulness isn't just about meditation or being present in the moment; it's about developing a profound understanding of your own thoughts and emotions. By practicing mindfulness, you've acquired the ability to observe your inner world without judgment, creating a space for self-reflection and growth. It also takes you on a journey of why DBT holds mindfulness in a higher regard and how you can incorporate the same in your life.

Furthermore, you've delved into the realm of emotional regulation, discovering how to manage intense feelings without letting them overpower you. These skills are essential for maintaining your emotional equilibrium, especially during those turbulent teenage years when emotions often run high. Chapter 4 further explores the activities that you can use to regulate your emotions.

Chapter 5 dealt with distress tolerance, which is an important skill to have when you are in a stressful situation. Remember, distress is an inevitable part of the human experience, but now, armed with the wisdom of DBT, you possess the ability to weather those storms without losing your footing. As you move forward on your journey, keep these valuable lessons close to your heart. So, face the future with courage, embrace your newfound resilience, and continue your journey toward a more balanced, fulfilling, and empowered life.

The chapter on interpersonal effectiveness has equipped you with the tools to navigate the complexities of human relationships. You've learned how to communicate effectively, set boundaries, and strike a balance between your needs and the needs of others. These skills are not only vital for building healthy relationships but also for establishing a strong sense of self and self-worth.

Throughout this journey, you've also explored the concept of acceptance. Life is full of uncertainties, and not everything will go according to plan. DBT teaches us that it's okay to acknowledge and accept these realities. Through radical acceptance, you've learned to embrace life on its terms, finding peace and resilience in the face of adversity.

Now, as we stand on the brink of concluding this informative and transformative adventure, remember that the journey doesn't end here; it's only just beginning. Life is an ever-evolving process, and the skills you've acquired through DBT are not just tools for the here and now but companions for a lifetime. You will find that your life is easier with these tools, but be sure to slowly incorporate them in your life. Do not overwhelm yourself by trying to pour everything into your routine all at once; instead, focus on taking one thing at a time.

The road ahead may still be challenging, and you may encounter obstacles and setbacks. However, armed with the wisdom of DBT, you have the power to face these challenges with courage and resilience. It's okay to stumble; it's okay to ask for help when needed. What's important is that you have the knowledge and skills to rise stronger each time you fall.

As you navigate the path ahead, keep in mind the principles of mindfulness, emotional regulation, interpersonal effectiveness, and acceptance. These principles are not just concepts to be understood; they are practices to be lived. They are the threads that will weave a tapestry of a fulfilling and purposeful life.

In a nutshell, remember that you are not alone on this journey. Your experiences, struggles, and successes are shared by countless others who have walked a similar path. So, as you move forward, do so with confidence, knowing that you have the tools, the knowledge, and the resilience to thrive. Embrace each moment, celebrate your growth, and continue to write your own story—one that is guided by the principles of DBT and marked by strength, self-discovery, and the pursuit of a successful future. Don't let the challenges of teenage life overwhelm you. Try DBT for positive change! Start your journey of self-discovery and growth. This is your chance to make a difference in your life. Use the skills you've learned here to unlock your potential and build a brighter future!

REFERENCES

Ackerman, C. E., & Wilson, C. R. (2017, December 29). *Interpersonal Effectiveness: 9 Worksheets & Examples (+ PDF)*. Positive Psychology. Retrieved September 10, 2023, from https://positivepsychology.com/interpersonal-effectiveness/.

Ackerman, C. E., & Wilson, C. R. (2017, December 29). *Interpersonal Effectiveness: 9 Worksheets & Examples (+ PDF)*. Positive Psychology. Retrieved September 10, 2023, from https://positivepsychology.com/interpersonal-effectiveness/#google_vignette.

ADAA. (2009, October 28). *Children and Teens - Anxiety and Depression*. Anxiety and Depression Association of America, ADAA. Retrieved July 7, 2023, from https://adaa.org/find-help/by-demographics/children/children-teens.

American Psychological Association. (2014, February 11). *Are Teens Adopting Adults' Stress Habits?* American Psychological Association. Retrieved July 11, 2023, from https://www.apa.org/news/press/releases/stress/2013/stress-report.pdf.

Andrews, T. (2022, November 4). *How to Control Your Emotions: Try a Weekly Cry Session*. POPSUGAR. Retrieved September 5, 2023, from https://www.popsugar.com/fitness/i-control-my-emotions-with-weekly-cry-sessions-49002435.

Asamoah, T. (2020). *6 Common Triggers of Teen Stress*. Psycom.net. Retrieved July 11, 2023, from https://www.psycom.net/common-triggers-teen-stress.

Biswas, M. (2016, March 7). *How Practicing Distress Tolerance Helps You Achieve More*. Indus Net Technologies. Retrieved September 10, 2023, from https://www.indusnet.co.in/practicing-distress-tolerance-helps-achieve/.

Bonfil, A. (2014, September 9). *Mindfulness from a DBT Perspective — Cognitive Behavioral Therapy Los Angeles*. Cognitive Behavioral Therapy Los Angeles. Retrieved September 5, 2023, from https://cogbtherapy.com/cbt-blog/mindfulness-in-dbt.

Borchard, T. J. (2020). *Depression Symptoms in Teens: Why Today's Teens Are More Depressed Than Ever*. Discovery Mood & Anxiety Program. Retrieved July 11, 2023, from https://discoverymood.com/blog/todays-teens-depressed-ever/.

Carey, B. (2011, June 23). *Expert on Mental Illness Reveals Her Own Struggle*. The New York Times. Retrieved July 8, 2023, from https://www.nytimes.com/2011/06/23/health/23lives.html.

Cherry, K. (2022, September 2). *The Benefits of Mindfulness*. Verywell Mind. Retrieved September 5, 2023, from https://www.verywellmind.com/the-benefits-of-mindfulness-5205137.

Cherry, K. (2022, September 22). *What Is Mindfulness Meditation?* Verywell Mind. Retrieved September 5, 2023, from https://www.verywellmind.com/mindfulness-meditation-88369.

Cho, J. (2022, October 2). ... - YouTube. Retrieved September 5, 2023, from https://www.forbes.com/sites/jeenacho/2016/07/14/10-scientifically-proven-benefits-of-mindfulness-and-meditation/?sh=7a38498563ce.

Chowdhury, M. R., & Smith, W. (2019, August 13). *Emotional Regulation: 6 Key Skills to Regulate Emotions*. Positive Psychology. Retrieved September 5, 2023, from https://positivepsychology.com/emotion-regulation/#regulation.

Cleveland Clinic. (2022, April 19). *Dialectical Behavior Therapy (DBT): What It Is & Purpose*. Cleveland Clinic. Retrieved July 8, 2023, from https://my.clevelandclinic.org/health/treatments/22838-dialectical-behavior-therapy-dbt.

Corporate Finance Institute. (2018, November 8). *Communication - Importance of Good Communication Skills*. Corporate Finance Institute. Retrieved September 10, 2023, from https://corporatefinanceinstitute.com/resources/management/communication/.

Crumpler, C., Figueroa, W., & Levine, P. (2022, March 29). *What is Mindfulness: Benefits, How to Practice, and More*. Healthline. Retrieved September 5, 2023, from https://www.healthline.com/health/mind-body/what-is-mindfulness.

DBT Self Help. (n.d.). *Identifying & Describing Emotions*. DBT Self Help. Retrieved September 5, 2023, from https://dbtselfhelp.com/dbt-skills-list/emotion-regulation/identifying-describing-emotions/.

DBT Self Help. (2020). *Emotion Regulation*. DBT Self Help. Retrieved September 5, 2023, from https://dbtselfhelp.com/dbt-skills-list/emotion-regulation/.

DBT.tools. (2020). *Distress Tolerance Skills - Dialectical Behavior Therapy (DBT) Tools*. DBT.tools. Retrieved September 10, 2023, from https://dbt.tools/distress_tolerance/index.php.

DBT.tools. (2020). *Interpersonal Effectiveness Skills - Dialectical Behavior Therapy (DBT) Tools*. DBT.tools. Retrieved September 10, 2023, from https://dbt.tools/interpersonal_effectiveness/index.php.

Dialectical Behavior Therapy. (2020). *DBT: Wise Mind - Skills, Worksheets, Videos, & Activities*. Dialectical Behavior Therapy. Retrieved September 5, 2023, from https://dialecticalbehaviortherapy.com/mindfulness/wise-mind/.

Dialectical Behavior Therapy. (2020). *RESISTT Technique : DBT*. Dialectical Behavior Therapy. Retrieved September 10, 2023, from https://dialecticalbehaviortherapy.com/distress-tolerance/resistt/.

Dialectical Behavior Therapy. (2022). *Emotion Exposure: DBT*. Dialectical Behavior Therapy. Retrieved September 5, 2023, from https://dialecticalbehaviortherapy.com/emotion-regulation/emotion-exposure/.

Eddins, R. (2017, September 21). *DBT and Your Teen: 7 Ways Teens Benefit from DBT Treatment*. Eddins Counseling Group. Retrieved July 11, 2023, from https://eddinscounseling.com/teens-benefit-dbt-treatment/.

Footprints Community. (2020). *Introduction to Dialectal Behavioural Therapy: The TIPP Skill | Footprints*. Footprints Community. Retrieved September 10, 2023, from https://footprintscommunity.org.au/resources/introduction-to-dialectal-behavioural-therapy-the-tipp-skill.

Geall, L. (n.d.). *Does mindfulness meditation actually work? One sceptic tries it*. Stylist. Retrieved September 5, 2023, from https://www.stylist.co.uk/life/mindfulness-meditation-does-it-work-wellbeing-self-care/379453.

Glosson, M. (2022, July 6). *Here Are My 5 Favorite Distress Tolerance Techniques and How I Use Them*. The Mighty. Retrieved September 10, 2023, from https://themighty.com/topic/borderline-personality-disorder/mental-health-how-to-use-distress-tolerance-techniques/.

Harris, A. (2022, June 8). *10 Steps of Radical Acceptance | DBT Skills*. HopeWay. Retrieved September 10, 2023, from https://hopeway.org/blog/radical-acceptance.

Harvard Health. (2023, February 23). *Benefits of Mindfulness*. HelpGuide.org. Retrieved September 5, 2023, from https://www.helpguide.org/harvard/benefits-of-mindfulness.htm.

Jacoby, S. (2021, June 22). Selena Gomez Practices This Type of Therapy Every Day. Retrieved July 11, 2023, from https://www.self.com/story/selena-gomez-therapy-every-day.

Jouany, V. (2023, January 22). *Interpersonal Communication: Definition, Importance and Must Have Skills*. Haiilo. Retrieved September 10, 2023, from https://haiilo.com/blog/interpersonal-communication-definition-importance-and-must-have-skills/.

Juby, B. (2022, September 30). *What is Emotional Self-Regulation and How You Develop It*. Healthline. Retrieved September 5, 2023, from https://www.healthline.com/health/emotional-self-regulation#about-emotional-self-regulation.

Klein, A. (2021, July 27). *Teen anxiety and depression: Causes, symptoms, and more*. Medical News Today. Retrieved July 11, 2023, from https://www.medicalnewstoday.com/articles/teen-anxiety-and-depression#causes.

Koonce, D. (2018, June 3). *Using Opposite Action for Overwhelming Emotions — Mindsoother Therapy Center*. Mindsoother Therapy Center. Retrieved September 5, 2023, from https://www.mindsoother.com/blog/using-opposite-action-for-overwhelming-emotions.

Lee, A., & Gottlieb, B. (2018, January 17). *DBT 101: What is Mindfulness?* Sheppard Pratt. Retrieved September 5, 2023, from https://www.sheppardpratt.org/news-views/story/dbt-101-what-is-mindfulness/.

Linehan, M. (2016, March 9). *Marsha Linehan Biography*. GoodTherapy. Retrieved July 8, 2023, from https://www.goodtherapy.org/famous-psychologists/marsha-linehan.html.

Love Wellness. (2020, September 25). *Using the 21/90™ Rule to Develop Good Habits*. Love Wellness. Retrieved September 10, 2023, from https://lovewellness.com/blogs/love-wellness/love-wellness-21-90-rule.

Mindfulness Therapy Associates. (2022). *The Core Skills of DBT: Wise Mind*. Mindfulness Therapy Associates. Retrieved September 5, 2023, from https://mindfulnesstherapy.org/wise-mind/.

Morin, A. (2020, June 29). *10 Signs Your Teen Is Stressed Out*. Verywell Mind. Retrieved July 11, 2023, from https://www.verywellmind.com/signs-your-teen-is-stressed-out-2611336.

My Health Alberta. (2019). *Learning About Stress in Teens*. My Health Alberta. Retrieved July 11, 2023, from https://myhealth.alberta.ca/Health/aftercareinformation/pages/conditions.aspx?hwid=ug6036.

Nasca, C. (2021). *4 Ways To Use Dialectical Behavioral Therapy Daily*. Anxiety.org. Retrieved September 10, 2023, from https://www.anxiety.org/dialectical-behavioral-therapy-dbt-simple-tips-steps.

Newport Academy. (2022, March 18). *Teen Stress and Stress Management*. Newport Academy. Retrieved July 11, 2023, from https://www.newportacademy.com/resources/mental-health/teen-stress-relief/.

Newroads. (2018, February 2). *Annie's Story: A Healing Journey with DBT (Dialectical Behavior Therapy)*. New Roads Behavioral Health. Retrieved September 10, 2023, from https://newroadstreatment.org/annies-story-a-healing-journey-with-dbt/.

Onque, R. (2023, March 2). *#DBT is trending on TikTok: 4 skills from the therapy practice*. CNBC. Retrieved July 8, 2023, from https://www.cnbc.com/2023/03/02/dbt-is-trending-on-tiktok-4-skills-from-the-therapy-practice.html.

PR Newswire. (2020, June 17). *New Survey Finds 7 in 10 Teens Are Struggling with Mental Health*. PR Newswire. Retrieved July 11, 2023, from https://www.prnewswire.com/news-releases/new-survey-finds-7-in-10-teens-are-struggling-with-mental-health-301078336.html.

Psychology Today. (2021). *Emotion Regulation*. Psychology Today. Retrieved September 5, 2023, from https://www.psychologytoday.com/us/basics/emotion-regulation.

ReachOut Parents. (2020). *Stress and teenagers*. ReachOut Parents. Retrieved July 11, 2023, from https://parents.au.reachout.com/common-concerns/everyday-issues/stress-and-teenagers.

Rosenthal, J. (2023, May 11). *Guide To DBT Distress Tolerance Skills | TIPP Skills*. Manhattan Psychology Group. Retrieved September 10, 2023, from https://manhattanpsychologygroup.com/dbt-tipp-skills/.

Saripalli, V., Carrico, B., & Linehan, M. (2021, June 15). *Dialectical Behavior Therapy for Anxiety and More I Psych Central*. Psych Central. Retrieved July 7, 2023, from https://psychcentral.com/lib/dialectical-behavior-therapy-for-more-than-borderline-personality-disorder.

Schimelpfening, N. (2023, May 1). *Dialectical Behavior Therapy (DBT): Definition, Techniques, and Benefits*. Verywell Mind. Retrieved July 8, 2023, from https://www.verywellmind.com/dialectical-behavior-therapy-1067402#toc-what-is-dbt-used-for.

Schimelpfening, N. (2023, May 1). *Dialectical Behavior Therapy (DBT): Definition, Techniques, and Benefits.* Verywell Mind. Retrieved July 8, 2023, from https://www.verywellmind.com/dialectical-behavior-therapy-1067402#toc-benefits-of-dbt.

Schimelpfening, N. (2023, May 1). *Dialectical Behavior Therapy (DBT): Definition, Techniques, and Benefits.* Verywell Mind. Retrieved July 8, 2023, from https://www.verywellmind.com/dialectical-behavior-therapy-1067402.

The Scientific World. (2020, December 27). *The Importance of Communication Skills in Everyday Life.* The Scientific World. Retrieved September 10, 2023, from https://www.scientificworldinfo.com/2020/12/importance-of-communication-skills-in-everyay-life.html.

Scott, E. (2021, September 13). *Why and How to Do a Mental Body Scan for Stress Relief.* Verywell Mind. Retrieved September 5, 2023, from https://www.verywellmind.com/body-scan-meditation-why-and-how-3144782.

Scott, E. (2022, December 1). *What Is Mindfulness?* Verywell Mind. Retrieved September 5, 2023, from https://www.verywellmind.com/mindfulness-the-health-and-stress-relief-benefits-3145189.

Smith, A. (2019). *DBT Success Stories — My Dialectical Life.* My Dialectical Life. Retrieved September 10, 2023, from https://www.mydialecticallife.com/dbt-success-stories.

Steinberg, L. (2021). *Anxiety and Depression in Adolescence.* Child Mind Institute. Retrieved July 7, 2023, from https://childmind.org/awareness-campaigns/childrens-mental-health-report/2017-childrens-mental-health-report/anxiety-depression-in-adolescence/.

Taylor, R. B. (2022, April 1). *Dialectical Behavioral Therapy for Mental Health Problems.* WebMD. Retrieved July 8, 2023, from https://www.webmd.com/mental-health/dialectical-behavioral-therapy.

Tull, M. (2020, July 17). *What Is Distress Tolerance?* Verywell Mind. Retrieved September 10, 2023, from https://www.verywellmind.com/distress-tolerance-2797294#toc-what-is-distress-tolerance.

Tull, M. (2020, July 17). *What Is Distress Tolerance?* Verywell Mind. Retrieved September 10, 2023, from https://www.verywellmind.com/distress-tolerance-2797294#toc-impact.

Van Dijk, S. (2021). *Self-Validation: DBT.* Dialectical Behavior Therapy. Retrieved September 5, 2023, from https://dialecticalbehaviortherapy.com/emotion-regulation/self-validation/.

Westside DBT. (2021). *5 Simple Mindfulness Practices for Daily Life – Westside DBT.* Westside DBT. Retrieved September 10, 2023, from https://westsidedbt.com/5-simple-mindfulness-practices-for-daily-life/.

Yeheyes, T. (2018, February 4). *Maya Angelou, Legendary Poet and Civil Rights Activist Who Had Disability, Inspires Generations.* RespectAbility. Retrieved July 11, 2023, from https://www.respectability.org/2018/02/maya-angelou-legendary-poet-civil-rights-activist-disability-inspires-generations/.

Made in the USA
Las Vegas, NV
27 March 2024

87817687R00063